WITHOUT A MAP

Searching For Who You Are

The Cover Story
The surrealistic cover photo was done by Scott Morgan. Scott designs a set for his photo the way the stage is arranged for a play. The floor and walls are arranged with the textures and colors he wants, objects are suspended from the ceiling or placed on the floor and walls, and light is directed to certain areas. Then he shoots his photo of the set.

ISBN: 0-673-80084-9

Copyright © 1993
Scott, Foresman and Company, Glenview, Illinois
All Rights Reserved.
Printed in the United States of America.

Acknowledgments appear on page 144.

345678910RRS99989796959493

WITHOUT A MAP

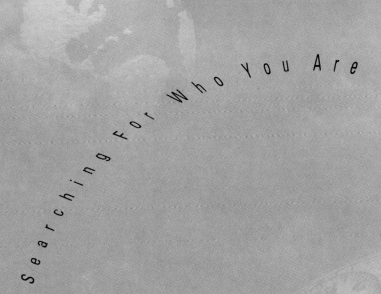

Searching For Who You Are

ScottForesman
A Division of HarperCollins*Publishers*

CONTENTS

Where Am I Going?

NOT YOUR AVERAGE FRESHMAN

by Bill Brittain

My first day as a freshman at Joseph P. Alewood High School was . . . Never in my whole life have I had a day like . . . It was as if I had . . .

Let me tell you about it. Then you'll understand what I mean.

I got up scared, ate my breakfast terrified, picked up my brand-new notebook and a handful of pens and pencils in a panic; and by the time I got to the corner and met Norma and Buster to wait for the school bus, I was trembling so hard I almost shook myself out of my shoes.

All the way to school, the bus driver gave us little lectures over his shoulder about how we were supposed to behave. Once we got there, the freshmen were herded onto the front lawn like a flock of sheep, with the sophomores, juniors and especially the seniors looking at us like we were wads of used chewing gum stuck to their shoes.

Then the whole freshman class was led into the auditorium for more lectures. Mr. Kipp, the principal, told us he expected great things of us, and the head of each of the departments told us his or her subject was the most important one we would ever have, and then one of the coaches kind of hinted that anybody who didn't at least try out for a team sport was a cowardly cream puff, and finally a guidance counselor who had a look on his face mean enough to etch glass said he wanted to be our friend.

Then we got paraded to our homerooms. Mine was for last names M-N-O-P, and except for a few kids I'd been in eighth grade with, everybody was a stranger. But I did have Norma Nagle sitting right behind me in the second row. As soon as we sat down—in strict alphabetical order—she began whispering to me.

"Isn't this *fun,* Stanley?"

Fun? I was a nobody! Just a name on a list.

Ms. Axton, the homeroom teacher, had just started her own lecture about being on time and what to do if you were absent. Suddenly a bell clanged. I guess this was the signal for the upper classes to move around, because all of a sudden faces began appearing at the window in the door of the room. They all had nasty grins, like Bela Lugosi in *Dracula,* and one or two of 'em even dragged their fingers across their throats in a slitting motion.

Well, if the older kids were trying to scare me, all I can say is, they were succeeding beyond their wildest hopes.

After her lecture, Ms. Axton gave us each a blue sheet with a locker number and combination, and a pink sheet with a list of the periods, rooms and classes we'd be taking.

"May I have your attention!" The voice coming from the loudspeaker sounded exactly like Claude Rains's in *The Invisible Man.*

"Freshman students will now move to your first period classes. You will ignore the bells. Listen for the announcements of class changes. You will move quickly and quietly."

Ms. Axton went to the door, opened it and threw us to the wolves. Fortunately the wolves were all in class when we freshmen hit the halls. I looked at my pink schedule list.

Per. 1 *Room 322*
SCIENCE *Mr. Bovinski*

After getting lost twice, I finally arrived at the science room five minutes late. Mr. Bovinski, who was kind of fat, with a bald head and a little wispy beard, steered me to a seat without missing a word of still another lecture.

"Now that you know the rules of this class,"

he said, "let's consider our first problem in general science—the conservation of energy."

I didn't have any idea what he was talking about. All we ever did in elementary school science was collect leaves and birds' nests. With a little groan, I put my head down on the desk and closed my eyes.

All of a sudden, the little gold man I'd seen in my dreams floated in the darkness. He was holding out all four of his hands to me.

"Who can give me an example of the law of conservation of energy?" Mr. Bovinski's voice seemed a long way off.

"You there, in the first row. Can you give me an answer?"

"No, Mr. Binky."

The gold man's arms moved up and down before my closed eyes like the waves of the sea. Up . . . down . . .

"Conservation of energy. It's very simple. How about you?" he said to another kid.

No answer. The gold man held things in each of his four hands—things that wafted through the air. Up . . . down . . .

"Or you." Mr. Bovinski's voice got louder. "Surely at least one person in this room can—"

Then I recognized what the gold man was playing with.

"Yo-yos!" I shouted.

"You! What's your name?" My eyes snapped open. Mr. Bovinski was pointing a finger at me like a loaded gun.

"Sta-Sta-Stanley. Stanley Muffet." I was going to die, for sure. "But Mr. Bovinski, all I said was—"

"You said 'yo-yos.' A perfect example of energy conservation. The energy invested in flinging the yo-yo *down* helps to bring it back *up*." He scribbled something into a book on his desk. "An A plus for today, Muffet. Keep up the good work." The loud groans and cries of "Teacher's pet!" from the rest of the class were drowned out by the loudspeaker announcing the end of the first period.

Per. 2 *Room 210*
MATHEMATICS *Ms. Darker*

I got to the room with plenty of time to spare and took a decent seat, way in the back. Ms. Darker, who didn't look old enough to drive a car, let alone teach school, had a l-o-n-g equation scribbled on the blackboard.

$$B = [4(14 - 23) + 71(13 \times 48) - (492 - 4)] \times 0(3 - 1728)$$

Below it were scribbled the words *Solve for B*. We all started messing around with pencils and paper, trying to look like we were working hard. The truth was none of us could any more solve the thing than we could fly. But we had to look busy, didn't we?

I scribbled a bunch of Z's— ZZZZZZZZZZZ—like somebody snoring. Then I sat back to admire my work. "The mark of Zorro!" I whispered, figuring I was safe enough way in the back.

But that Ms. Darker must have had ears like a jackrabbit's. "Repeat that, please," she commanded, skewering me with her icicle gaze.

"Zorro!" I said in confusion. "I mean
zero . . . uh . . . nothing."
"Zero—or nothing!" she cried out trium-
phantly. "Look at that last factor, class. Zero times
anything is zero. Well done—uh—what's your
name?" She leaned over her class book.
Another A+ for yours truly, Stanley Muffet.

Per. 3 Room 261
SOCIAL STUDIES Mrs. Cobb

Mrs. Cobb had to be at least seventy years
old, skinny and frail. But the no-nonsense look on
her face seemed to say that anybody who tried
something with her had better be backed up by at
least six combat-ready Marines.
She began with a few really easy questions
about American history. But I kept my hand down
and let the others answer. I'd done enough
showing off for one day. Finally she let fly with
a question that stumped just about everyone.
"Name three heroes of the Battle of
the Alamo."
Nobody could do it. Nobody except me.
At home, I'd watched The Alamo, with John
Wayne, Richard Widmark and Laurence Harvey at
least a dozen times. Cool as a dish of orange
sherbet, I raised my hand.
"Davy Crockett, Jim Bowie and William
Travis!" I piped up.
Mrs. Cobb peered at me over the tops of her
glasses. "You will refrain from shouting answers
before being called upon," she told me in a voice
like fingernails scraping on a blackboard.

"Yes, ma'am."

"But your reply is entirely correct. Your name, please?"

And what do you think Mrs. Cobb put down in *her* mark book?

Per. 4 *Cafeteria*
LUNCH

This is the period when I thought my luck had run out and I was really in trouble. Let me tell you.

At the cafeteria I got in a line about a mile long, but finally I got my food. It was okay, if you don't mind frankfurters that taste like lumber and library-paste baked beans.

When I'd finished, I decided to find my locker and see if I could open it and stash some of the armful of opening-day announcements I'd been hauling around all morning.

I located my locker, but working the combination was something else again. I tried it three times, but the metal door just sat there locked, laughing at me. Down the hall a couple of other freshmen were having troubles of their own with their lockers.

I got so mad at that closed door I finally gave it a good swift kick, and that's when I felt the tap on my shoulder and heard that sneering, holier-than-thou voice.

"Hey, frosh."

"Who?" I turned around. There stood a tall, skinny, red-haired boy, maybe three years older than me, wearing a dirty shirt, a necktie that must have been a grease rag once and an expression on his face like he'd just swallowed a rotten prune. Next to him was another boy, about the size and shape of a piano crate, with a face a mule would have been ashamed of.

"Are you talking to me?" I asked.

"You got it, frosh," said dirty shirt. "I'm Jerry Frye—*Mister* Frye to you—and this is Stonewall Lugg. We're the senior welcoming committee. And we don't like the lowly freshmen kicking the locker doors. You might hurt 'em. Right, Stonewall?"

"Yeah," said Stonewall. As soon as I heard him, I knew he had an I.Q. of about 6. But those arms of his could crush me like a grape.

"Tell the door you're sorry, frosh," Jerry Frye ordered with a smirk. "Otherwise you get this whole can of soda poured all over you."

He pulled a can of Pepsi from behind his back and jiggled it around like it was a pistol or a knife. A couple of spoonfuls slopped out and dribbled onto the hallway floor.

By this time a dozen or so big guys had gathered behind Frye and Lugg to see what was going on. I looked up and down the hallway. Not a teacher in sight.

I wasn't about to go through the rest of the day wringing Pepsi-Cola out of my sweater and socks. So I turned to the door.

"I'm sorry, door," I said, feeling like an idiot.

"Now give the door a kiss," Jerry ordered.

"Yeah. Make friends," added Stonewall.

They were nuttier than a fruitcake. But what was I supposed to do?

I kissed the door.

"Very good, frosh. Now I won't have to pour this soda over your head."

"Well thanks, very . . ."

"I'm gonna pour it in your pocket, instead."
Jerry reached out, yanked my pants pocket open
with one hand and started tipping the can, which
was in the other. That dirty tie he had on swung
back and forth like wash on a line.

"Hey, wait a minute!" I howled. "You can't—"
I tried to dodge to one side. That's when my
heel came down on the spot of spilled soda. My
foot skidded, and I lost my balance. I reached
desperately for something—anything—that
would keep me from falling flat on my back on
the hard tile.

I grabbed hold of Jerry Frye's necktie and held
on for dear life. The knot slid, and the loop of tie
around his neck pulled tighter and tighter. Jerry
dropped the can of Pepsi and yanked at the collar
of his shirt. His face turned red . . . then
blue . . . then purple.

Finally the tie slid through my fingers, and I
dropped onto my rear end. I covered my head
with my arms, just waiting for Stonewall Lugg to
land on me and start caving in my ribs with those
big fists of his. I hoped I'd die fast.

Nothing happened. Finally I chanced a peek up
at Stonewall.

He was pointing at Jerry Frye and laughing his
head off. All the other guys standing around were
laughing too. Jerry's eyes were bulging out, and he
was trying to shout. But with that tie pulled tight
around his neck, he could hardly breathe, much
less talk.

Finally a teacher showed up—an old one,
wearing glasses and a sport coat that should have
been a horse blanket. He took in what was going
on, choked back a laugh of his own and tried to

loosen Jerry's tie. But it was stuck tight.

The teacher took a knife from his pocket and cut the tie loose.

For a moment Jerry just stood there, gasping for breath. Then he seemed to hear the laughter for the first time.

"Hey, cut it out," he gasped. "There's nothing funny. This frosh could have killed me."

"A small loss that the world could easily afford," said the teacher. "Up to your old tricks of hazing the new students, Mr. Frye?"

While everybody's attention was on Jerry Frye, it seemed like a good time for me to make my escape. I started tiptoeing off down the hall.

"Jerry Frye, licked by a little ol' freshman," hooted someone. "This oughta make page one when the school paper comes out."

"Hey, you! Frosh!" Jerry bellowed at me. "Come back here!"

Even Dexter Dragon, who's got stuffing where his brains should be, would know better than to obey *that* order. I broke into a run.

"You just wait, frosh." By now, Jerry was screaming. "Sooner or later, I'm gonna find you when there's not a teacher standing around. Then I'm gonna turn you inside out and tie you in knots. Nobody makes me look like a fool."

"Somebody already did," I heard a girl giggle from the end of the hall. "You've bullied a lot of people in this school, Jerry Frye. When this story gets around, that frosh is going to be a hero."

Me, a hero? Hey, I'd been in school only half a day, and already things were looking up.

But I couldn't help wondering what would happen the next time Jerry Frye and I came face to face. What good is it being a hero if you're dead?

Per. 5 *Gymnasium*
PHYSICAL EDUCATION *Mr. Elkins*

The less said about gym class, the better. I'm not the physical type. But that first day, Coach Elkins just passed around a bunch of lists. I didn't know what they were for, but I signed every one I could get my hands on. Hey, how was I going to get to be a VIP if I didn't have my name plastered all over the school?

Per. 6 *Room 302*
ENGLISH *Mr. Smee*

Short, fat Mr. Smee began the class by reading us a quote from Shakespeare's *Hamlet*— "To be or not to be. ..." Then he told us to write a paragraph of seventy-five words or less about what it meant.

I hadn't any idea. Maybe Hamlet didn't know what word to use in a sentence he was writing. Maybe he'd forgotten the number of his hotel room. Or maybe...

I just couldn't make up my mind. And that's exactly what I told Mr. Smee in my paragraph.

When he read some of the paragraphs to the class, Mr. Smee went absolutely *ape* over mine. "You've summed up Hamlet's problem in a nutshell, Mr. Muffet," he gloated. "The Melancholy Dane simply couldn't make up his mind. And Muffet, your use of the first person—writing as if you were the hero of the story—is a stroke of genius."

I was leading a charmed life. And I was loving it!

Per. 7 *Room 119*
ART *Mr. Pinkerton*

With everything that'd happened before, do you really need to know about art class? Do you really want me to tell you how Mr. Pinkerton— tall and with an English accent that made all the girls swoon—picked out my paper full of crayon scrawls and how he told the class art wasn't photography and my work reminded him of the great impressionist painters like Van Gogh and Manet?

Of course you don't. Enough is enough.

Per. 8 *Room 325*
STUDY HALL

Three seniors came up to me especially to say hello. They told me I was real brave because of what I'd done to Jerry Frye, which is what they'd always wanted to do but were scared to because Jerry always hung around with Stonewall Lugg.

One senior girl thought I was cute.

All the way home on the school bus that afternoon I kept gloating about my first day at Joseph P. Alewood High School. I was at the top of all my classes. I'd licked the school bully. Three seniors—maybe a lot more—knew who I was. At this rate, I'd be a VIP in no time.

Thinking
About**it**

1. Does Stanley Muffet's first day of high school trigger any memories? What happened to *you* on your first day—*any* first day—of school? What would Stanley say of your first day?

2. Is Stanley Muffet really VIP (Very Important Person) material, or is he really just your average freshman? Find the parts of the story that support your choice.

3. Suppose that when Stanley grows up, he becomes a principal. (Such things *do* happen sometimes.) What is his plan of action? Specifically, what does he do to help run the school on opening day?

Another Book About Handling Problems

Stanley's problems seem to resolve themselves, but you know that that isn't reality. *Where's My Other Sock? How to Get Organized and Drive Your Parents and Teachers Crazy* by Wirths and Bowman-Kruhm will help you save time and organize your things.

THE WAR OF THE WALL

by Toni Cade Bambara

Me and Lou had no time for courtesies.
We were late for school. So we just flat
out told the painter lady to quit messing
with the wall. It was our wall, and she had
no right coming into our neighborhood
painting on it. Stirring in the paint bucket
and not even looking at us, she mumbled
something about Mr. Eubanks, the barber,
giving her permission. That had nothing to

do with it as far as we were concerned. We've been pitching pennies against that wall since we were little kids. Old folks have been dragging their chairs out to sit in the shade of the wall for years. Big kids have been playing handball against the wall since so-called integration when the crazies 'cross town poured cement in our pool so we couldn't use it. I'd sprained my neck one time boosting my cousin Lou up to chisel Jimmy Lyon's name into the wall when we found out he was never coming home from the war in Vietnam to take us fishing.

"If you lean close," Lou said, leaning hipshot against her beat-up car, "you'll get a whiff of bubble gum and kids' sweat. And that'll tell you something—that this wall belongs to the kids of Taliaferro Street." I thought Lou sounded very convincing. But the painter lady paid us no mind. She just snapped the brim of her straw hat down and hauled her bucket up the ladder.

"You're not even from around here," I hollered up after her. The license plates on her old piece of car said "New York." Lou dragged me away because I was about to grab hold of that ladder and shake it. And then we'd really be late for school.

When we came from school, the wall was slick with white. The painter lady was running string across the wall and taping it here and there. Me and Lou leaned against the gum ball machine outside the pool hall and watched. She had strings up and down and back and forth. Then she began chalking them with a hunk of blue chalk.

The Morris twins crossed the street, hanging back at the curb next to the beat-up car. The twin with the red ribbons was hugging a jug of cloudy lemonade. The one with yellow ribbons was holding a plate of dinner away from her dress. The painter lady began snapping the strings. The blue chalk dust measured off halves and quarters up and down and sideways too. Lou was about to say how hip it all was, but I dropped my book satchel on his toes to remind him we were at war.

Some good aromas were drifting our way from the plate leaking pot likker onto the Morris girl's white socks. I could tell from where I stood that under the tinfoil was baked ham, collard greens, and candied yams. And knowing Mrs. Morris, who sometimes bakes for my mama's restaurant, a slab of buttered cornbread was probably up under there too, sopping up some of the pot likker. Me and Lou rolled our eyes, wishing somebody would send us some dinner. But the painter lady didn't even turn around. She was pulling the strings down and prying bits of tape loose.

Side Pocket came strolling out of the pool hall to see what Lou and me were studying so hard. He gave the painter lady the once-over, checking out her paint-spattered jeans, her chalky T-shirt, her floppy-brimmed straw hat. He hitched up his pants and glided over toward the painter lady who kept right on with what she was doing.

"Watcha got there, Sweetheart?" he asked the twin with the plate.

"Suppah," she said all soft and country-like.

"For her," the one with the jug added, jerking her chin toward the painter lady's back.

Still she didn't turn around. She was rearing back on her heels, her hands jammed into her back pockets, her face squinched up like the master-piece she had in mind was taking shape on the wall by magic. We could have been gophers crawled up into a rotten hollow for all she cared. She didn't even say hello to anybody. Lou was muttering something about how great her concentration was. I butt him with my hip, and his elbow slid off the gum machine.

"Good evening," Side Pocket said in his best ain't-I-fine voice. But the painter lady was moving from the milk crate to the stepstool to the ladder, moving up and down fast, scribbling all over the wall like a crazy person. We looked at Side Pocket. He looked at the twins. The twins looked at us. The painter lady was giving a show. It was like those old-timey music movies where the dancer taps on the table top and then starts jumping all over the furniture, kicking chairs over and not skipping a beat. She didn't even look where she was stepping. And for a minute there, hanging on the ladder to reach a far spot, she looked like she was going to tip right over.

"Ahh," Side Pocket cleared his throat and moved fast to catch the ladder. "These young ladies here have brought you some supper."

"Ma'am?" The twins stepped forward. Finally the painter turned around, her eyes "full of sky" as my grandmama would say. Then she stepped down like she was in a trance. She wiped her hands on her jeans as the Morris twins offered up the plate and the jug. She rolled back the tinfoil, then wagged her head as though something terrible was on the plate.

"Thank your mother very much," she said, sounding like her mouth was full of sky too. "I've brought my own dinner along." And then, without even excusing herself, she went back up the ladder, drawing on the wall in a wild way. Side Pocket whistled one of those oh-brother breathy whistles and went back into the pool hall. The Morris twins shifted their weight from one foot to the other, then crossed the street and went home. Lou had to drag me away, I was so mad. We couldn't wait to get to the firehouse to tell my daddy all about this rude woman who'd stolen our wall.

All the way back to the block to help my mama out at the restaurant, me and Lou kept asking my daddy for ways to run the painter lady out of town. But my daddy was busy talking about the trip to the country and telling Lou he could come too because Grandmama can always use an extra pair of hands on the farm.

Later that night, while me and Lou were in the back doing our chores, we found out that the painter lady was a liar. She came into the restaurant and leaned against the glass of the steam table talking about how starved she was. I was scrubbing pots and Lou was chopping onions, but we could hear her through the service window. She was asking Mama was that a ham hock in the greens, and was that a neck bone in the pole beans, and were there any vegetables cooked without meat, especially pork.

"I don't care who your spiritual leader is," Mama said in that way of hers. "If you eat in the community, sistuh, you gonna eat pig by-and-by, one way or t'other."

Me and Lou were cracking up in the kitchen, and several customers at the counter were clearing their throats waiting for Mama to really fix her wagon for not speaking to the elders when she came in. The painter lady took a stool at the counter and went right on with her questions. Was there cheese in the baked macaroni, she wanted to know? Were there eggs in the salad? Was it honey or sugar in the iced tea? Mama was fixing Pop Johnson's plate. And every time the painter lady asked a fool question, Mama would dump another spoonful of rice on the pile. She was tapping her foot and heating up in a dangerous way. But Pop Johnson was happy as he could be. Me and Lou peeked though the service window, wondering what planet the painter lady came from. Who ever heard of baked macaroni without cheese, or potato salad without eggs?

"Do you have any bread made with un-bleached flour?" the painter lady asked Mama. There was a long pause as though everybody in the restaurant was holding their breath, wondering if Mama would dump the next spoonful on the painter lady's head. She didn't. But when she set Pop Johnson's plate down, it came down with a bang.

When Mama finally took her order, the starv-ing lady all of a sudden couldn't make up her mind whether she wanted a vegetable plate or fish and a salad. She finally settled on the broiled trout and a tossed salad. But just when Mama reached for a plate to serve her, the painter lady leaned over the counter with her finger all up in the air.

"Excuse me," she said. "One more thing." Mama was holding the plate like a Frisbee, tapping that foot, one hand on her hip. "Can I get raw beets in that tossed salad?"

"You will get," Mama said, leaning her face close to the painter lady's, "whatever Lou back there tossed. Now sit down." And the painter lady sat back down on her stool and shut right up.

All the way to the country, me and Lou tried to get Mama to open fire on the painter lady. But Mama said that seeing as how she was from the North, you couldn't expect her to have any manners. Then Mama said she was sorry she'd been so impatient with the woman because she seemed like a decent person and was simply trying to stick to a very strict diet. Me and Lou didn't want to hear that. Who did that lady think she was, coming into our neighborhood and taking over our wall?

"Wellllll," Mama drawled, pulling into the filling station so Daddy could take the wheel, "it's hard on an artist, ya know. They can't always get people to look at their work. So she's just doing her work in the open, that's all."

Me and Lou definitely did not want to hear that. Why couldn't she set up an easel downtown or draw on the sidewalk in her own neighborhood? Mama told us to quit fussing so much; she was tired and wanted to rest. She climbed into the back seat and dropped down into the warm hollow Daddy had made in the pillow.

All weekend long, me and Lou tried to scheme up ways to recapture our wall. Daddy and Mama said they were sick of hearing about it. Grandmama turned up the TV to drown us out. On the late news was a story about the New York subways. When a train came roaring into the station all covered from top to bottom, windows too, with writings and drawings done with spray

paint, me and Lou slapped five. Mama said it was
too bad kids in New York had nothing better to
do than spray paint all over the trains. Daddy said
that in the cities even grown-ups wrote all over
the trains and buildings too. Daddy called it
"graffiti." Grandmama called it a shame.

We couldn't wait to get out of school on
Monday. We couldn't find any black spray paint anywhere. But in a junky hardware store downtown
we found a can of white epoxy paint, the kind you
touch up old refrigerators with when they get
splotchy and peely. We spent our whole allowance
on it. And because it was too late to use our bus
passes, we had to walk all the way home lugging
our book satchels and gym shoes, and the bag with
the epoxy.

When we reached the corner of Taliaferro
and Fifth, it looked like a block party or something.
Half the neighborhood was gathered on the sidewalk in front of the wall. I looked at Lou, he
looked at me. We both looked at the bag with the
epoxy and wondered how we were going to work
our scheme. The painter lady's car was nowhere in
sight. But there were too many people standing
around to do anything. Side Pocket and his buddies
were leaning on their cue sticks, hunching each
other. Daddy was there with a lineman he catches
a ride with on Mondays. Mrs. Morris had her arms
flung around the shoulders of the twins on either
side of her. Mama was talking with some of her
customers, many of them with napkins still at the
throat. Mr. Eubanks came out of the barber shop,
followed by a man in a striped poncho, half his face
shaved, the other half full of foam.

"She really did it, didn't she?" Mr. Eubanks
huffed out his chest. Lots of folks answered right

quick that she surely did when they saw the straight razor in his hand.

Mama beckoned us over. And then we saw it. The wall. Reds, greens, figures outlined in black. Swirls of purple and orange. Storms of blues and yellows. It was something. I recognized some of the faces right off. There was Martin Luther King, Jr. And there was a man with glasses on and his mouth open like he was laying down a heavy rap. Daddy came up alongside and reminded us that he was Minister Malcolm X. The serious woman with a rifle I knew was Harriet Tubman because my grandmama has pictures of her all over the house. And I knew Mrs. Fannie Lou Hamer 'cause a signed photograph of her hangs in the restaurant next to the calendar.

Then I let my eyes follow what looked like a vine. It trailed past a man with a horn, a woman with a big white flower in her hair, a handsome dude in a tuxedo seated at a piano, and a man with a goatee holding a book. When I looked more closely, I realized that what had looked like flowers were really faces. One face with yellow petals looked just like Frieda Morris. One with red petals looked just like Hattie Morris. I could hardly believe my eyes.

"Notice," Side Pocket said, stepping close to the wall with his cue like a classroom pointer. "These are the flags of liberation," he said in a voice I'd never heard him use before. We all stepped closer while he pointed and spoke. "Red, black and green," he said, his pointer falling on the leaf-like flags of the vine. "Our liberation flag. And here Ghana, there Tanzania. Guinea-Bissau, Angola, Mozambique." Side Pocket sounded very tall, as though he'd been waiting all his life to give this lesson.

Mama tapped us on the shoulder and pointed to a high section of the wall. There was a fierce-looking man with his arms crossed against his chest guarding a bunch of children. His muscles bulged and he looked a lot like my daddy. One kid was looking at a row of books. Lou hunched me 'cause the kid looked like me. The one that looked like Lou was spinning a globe on the tip of his finger like a basketball. There were other kids there with microscopes and compasses. And the more I looked, the more it looked like the fierce man was not so much guarding the kids as defending their right to do what they were doing.

Then Lou gasped and dropped the paint bag and ran forward, running his hands over a rainbow. He had to tiptoe and stretch to do it, it was so high. I couldn't breathe either. The painter lady had found the chisel marks and had painted Jimmy Lyon's name in a rainbow.

"Read the inscription, honey," Mrs. Morris said, urging little Frieda forward. She didn't have to urge much. Frieda marched right up, bent down, and in a loud voice that made everybody quit oohing and ahhing and listen, she read,

To the People of Taliaferro Street
I Dedicate This Wall of Respect
Painted in Memory of My Cousin Jimmy Lyons

Outdoor Art In America

BY TONI CADE BAMBARA

In the 1940s, the Rheingold Beer Company started a contest. They would plaster posters of blondes and redheads all over buildings, buses, and highways asking the public to vote for the next Miss Rheingold. One day we found a huge metal grid in the vacant lot we used for play; the thing looked like a giant's easel. We knew it was not the playground equipment promised by the city's park and recreation division. A six-foot-square billboard of the new Miss Rheingold soon filled the grid. The city had decided to lease the lot to the beer company. Needless to say, I became a community organizer early.

During the 1960s, streets, parks, and other public spaces became the arena for millions of people determined to make democracy a reality for everyone in the country. Many of these determined people were activist artists of downpressed communities. They used their talents and skills to agitate and educate for social change. These poets, singers, and others shared their training by moving from the privacy of their studios and working outdoors. There it was easier to mobilize neighborhoods around issues of discrimination and exploitation, community and power.

A Chicago-based African American artist collective called Afrocobra was instrumental in sparking an outdoor art movement throughout the country; it was most immediately experienced in the national black community. Walls of respect were done collectively, in keeping with the emphasis placed on community. The spirit of the outdoor art movement was arts-for-people's-sake. This idea challenged the arts-for-art's-sake notion that art is valuable only when it is done by one "special" individual and is housed in a big museum.

In the 1970s, youths who drew or painted on

top of advertisements that cluttered their environment were called public artists by community people. The authorities called them criminals. To show that the city belonged, not just to corporations, but to young people too, these artists began practicing their craft in park tunnels, on bridges, and on trains. They risked arrest.

There's an incredible work of collective outdoor art called "The Great Wall of Los Angeles." It was executed in the 1980s by more than one hundred people. Under the directorship of Mexican American activist artist Judy Baca, the half-mile long mural depicts the history of California from the point of view of Native Americans and Mexican Americans. Unlike the walls of the 1960s, it is not set in the neighborhood of the artists.

Baca chose the wall of a flood channel in a very high-priced district of the San Fernando Valley. The artists were youths from working class neighborhoods of Los Angeles. Baca "sprang" many of them from juvenile detention centers where they'd been sentenced for art activity in tunnels, bridges, and trains. Warrior art I call it.

This warrior art, this rich heritage of outdoor art, led me to write "The War of the Wall." I wondered how people in the neighborhood would react if a stranger started painting on a wall, *their* wall. What reasons might the artist have for painting? What might be the subject of her painting? What would people do if the artist wouldn't talk to them? From these questions came my story.

Thinking About it

1. Why this war over a wall? When have you had a conflict like "The War of the Wall" over a possession or a territory? How did it turn out?

2. While you read "The War of the Wall," whose side were you on—the main character's or the "painter lady's"? Why? Did your feelings toward any of the characters change at the end of the story? Explain.

3. The woman painted the wall in memory of her cousin, who died in Vietnam. What other ways are there to keep the memory of a loved one alive?

Another Book About Misunderstanding Messages

You sometimes believe something you *want* to believe, and that's exactly what happens to Lexi and Jeb in *A Tribe for Lexi* by C. S. Adler. They *want* to believe that a small band of Indians is still living in the Catskills, and soon they're off on a perilous journey to unexpected places.

4 O'CLOCK ON Mondays and THURSDAYS

by Nicholasa Mohr

This morning I had gotten permission to go over to Gigi's house after school. Gigi's mother is the most easygoing mother I know. I am welcome to visit them anytime, just as long as I get Mami's okay. Gigi's mother even takes me shopping with them and buys me treats and lunch. I call her by her first name and so does Gigi. Before I used to call her Mrs.

Mercado, but last year she insisted I call her Doris. When I had told Mami that, she said she thought it was disrespectful, and that Mrs. Mercado must think she was Gigi's sister instead of her mother. But I don't care how Mami feels. I love being with Doris and Gigi because I can be myself. I can say whatever pops into my head and not have to worry about getting an argument back.

When we got to class, I sat next to Gigi and whispered the good news about my trip. Then I added, "Can I come over to your house after school? I got permission."

"Great." She nodded.

I could hardly keep my mind on my school-work, and when lunchtime came around, I was practically jumping out of my skin. We have our tight little group in school. There is Gigi, Consuela, Elba Thomas, Lydia Cortez, and Vivian Montañez. Today we all sat together like always. I waited for just the right moment, after everyone was settled and munching away.

"Guess what, everybody? I'm going to Puerto Rico for the whole summer!" I announced.

"Wow!" said Elba.

"Really? That's great!" Vivian said. Right away everybody became interested.

"When are you going exactly?" asked Lydia.

"Not until school is over. We're all leaving early in July. My parents and brothers are only staying two weeks, but I'm going to—"

"Oh, man, look! There he is. There's Vinny!" Vivian interrupted me, and everyone turned away to look at Vinny Davila as he walked by and waved at us.

"He's so cute," Vivian went on. "I just love his eyes." She kept on waving at him longer than anybody else with a smile stuck on her face and her teeth hanging out. I tried to get back their attention so I could talk about my trip, but now there was no way they would listen. Everyone was more interested in Vinny, the new boy from Colombia, South America. He had registered at our school only at the beginning of last month. His real name was Vicente Davila, but he had asked everyone to call him Vinny, which he pronounced "Veenie." Naturally we all knew he meant Vinny, but that Joey Ramos and his dumb gang of friends took advantage of him and made fun of him. They imitated his accent and called him "Beenie." That really made me mad.

Vinny's English was so bad that they put him back. That's why even though he's a year older than our group, he's in our grade. I heard he's the oldest of five kids. He lives right on my block so I usually see him walking to and from school, but so far I've never seen him hanging out. He has jet black hair and fair skin with freckles. All the girls think he's real cute. And even though I never said it, I gotta admit he's a very handsome boy. But I'm glad he's not in my class. You see, I really can't stand it when all my girlfriends act so silly over boys.

Like right now, for instance, here I am trying to say something important about my trip, and they all don't even care.

"Like I was saying," I went on. "My brothers are leaving early, which makes me happy. My Tio Jorge[1] says we'll be going for hikes and to the beach and—"

"Oh, look, here he comes again. Look!" Vivian cut me off a second time and began to giggle.

[1] Uncle Jorge

"He's coming our way. Oh, I can't stand it!" She kept right on grinning at him.

"I think you're the one he's looking at, Vivian," said Elba.

"I sure hope so." Vivian sighed. "Like who cares if his English stinks. I could teach him how to talk better real quick." All the girls began to laugh and were now grinning at Vinny like fools. All except Gigi. She just looked at me and rolled back her eyes. By now I was pretty furious. It was like what I had to say was not the least bit important because Vinny came around. All right, I thought, just wait until they all have something important they want me to hear. I'll show them.

"I guess you all are not interested in my trip or care about what I was saying." I looked directly at Vivian.

"Felita, you ain't even going until the summer," she said, "and we all got plenty of time to hear about your trip."

I was so annoyed at her. "Hey, I'm not twisting any arms, so you all don't have to listen. I only figured as my very best friends you'd like to hear about my good news. That's all!"

"We are interested, Felita," said Elba, "go on and tell us." I remained silent until they all had to ask me again.

"We're all ears," said Lydia.

"All right, then." I was too happy thinking about my trip to stay angry. But there wasn't much time left before lunch was over and we had to get back to class.

After school Gigi and I went over to her house. Last year her parents had bought a big apartment in a development that was a twenty-minute walk from school. It was drizzling out and the leftover snow was turning into rivers of brown mush and disappearing into the drain holes and sewers. The dampness and cold made us shiver. Gigi and I linked our arms and huddled together to keep warm. We walked so fast that we were practically running.

"Imagine, living in a place where it never gets cold," I said.

"I can't imagine," Gigi said. "Not on a day like today."

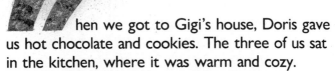

hen we got to Gigi's house, Doris gave us hot chocolate and cookies. The three of us sat in the kitchen, where it was warm and cozy.

"Bueno," Doris said, "what a lucky girl you are to be going on such a long vacation to Puerto Rico."

"I know." I sure was feeling pleased. "I already heard so many stories about P.R., ever since I was little. My abuelita[2] told me that everything is so beautiful—the flowers, mountains..."

[2]grandmother

"It's beautiful all right, but it's also changed a lot since your grandmother's time," said Doris. "I know because when I went there for a visit eight years ago, I found things were a whole lot different than when I was young."

"Oh, but you see, my Tio Jorge says that we'll be living in his village and that not much has changed there."

"What's the difference? I know you'll have a great time anyway, Felita."

"I wish I could go with Felita," said Gigi.

"Someday we're all going, but we just bought this apartment and you know your father and I can't afford any trips now. But we will have a family reunion in Puerto Rico one day, and you'll meet all your relatives there, Gigi. I promise."

"Great, Doris." Gigi kissed her mother. "When is Daddy coming home?"

"Thursday of next week. He wrote that he's bringing us something special." Gigi's father is a merchant seaman who is away for many weeks at a time. But when he comes home from a trip, it's so much fun, almost like having a celebration. He brings all kinds of pretty things for their home and gifts for Gigi and Doris. Sometimes he gives me something too. Last time I got a bottle of toilet water that smelled like roses.

After we finished eating, Gigi and I went to her room. She has such a big room. It's at least three times the size of my cubbyhole. They even have two bathrooms in their apartment. Would I love to have two bathrooms in my house! Everybody is always fighting to get to the toilet first, or waiting to get in. I can never sit down in peace without somebody banging on the door. In her room Gigi has her own portable color T.V.,

and last month her father got her a new
cassette player.

"You are so lucky, Gigi. I wish I had some of
the things you have. Especially my own T.V. Do
you know what a pain it is to watch programs
everybody else likes except you? When my brothers take over with their sports programs, it's like
nothing else matters."

"But it must be so nice to have two older
brothers. It gets lonely being an only child, you
know. Nobody to talk to or play with."

"Are you kidding? Who talks to my brothers?
Or plays with them? All they do is boss me around
and tell me what to do. Mostly we fight." I looked
around her room. "I wish I was an only child so I
could have all these great things for my very own
private use."

"I don't know, but sometimes I would trade
in all of this for a brother or sister. When I was
little, I always used to ask my parents for a baby
sister or brother. First they used to tell me that in
the future God would bring me one, but as I got
older and kept on asking, they finally told me the
truth. There was not gonna be any more kids in
this family, they told me. Like I was it. They said
that this way they could afford to give me the best
of everything, and that they just couldn't afford no
more kids."

"That sounds like a good idea to me. I could
do without Tito, even Johnny sometimes, and in
that order."

"Well"—Gigi shook her head—"I still wish I
had a sister."

"But you and I are sisters. Don't you remember the pact we made in first grade? We agreed
then that we would always be sisters, and so

we are."

"True." Gigi looked real sad. "I'm gonna miss you so much, Felita. I wish I could go with you." Now we both became quiet and sad, thinking about being separated.

"Wait a minute. I'm only going for the summer and I'm not even leaving till July, and it's only March. So why are we feeling so sad?"

"Right!" Gigi laughed, and we hugged.

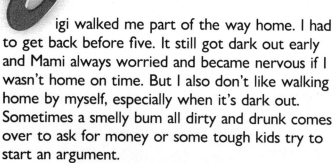 igi walked me part of the way home. I had to get back before five. It still got dark out early and Mami always worried and became nervous if I wasn't home on time. But I also don't like walking home by myself, especially when it's dark out. Sometimes a smelly bum all dirty and drunk comes over to ask for money or some tough kids try to start an argument.

Gigi and I said good-bye by the large boulevard, and I rushed across the street, putting on some speed.

"Felita! Mira, Felita, espera...espera un momento!" I heard my name and someone calling out to me in Spanish to wait up. Turning around, I saw Vinny Davila. He was waving as he hurried over. "Hello, are you going home?" he asked me in Spanish. I nodded. "Can I walk along with you, please?" "Sure." I shrugged. I wasn't expecting to see Vinny. It felt strange walking with Vinny because I hardly knew him or had ever really had a conversation with him. The rain had stopped and the sharp wind sent a chill right through my coat. Neither of us said anything. I kept waiting for him to say something, but he just walked silently alongside me. Finally I decided to break the ice by speaking first, in Spanish. "How do you like it in this country so far?"

"I like it." He smiled. "I'm learning and seeing new things every day." We continued to speak in Spanish.

"That's very good. Do you like school here?"

"Yes, except for my English, which is pretty lousy. I wanna work on it so that I can speak it fluently just like all the other kids."

"It must be hard to come here from another country and have to learn to speak a different language right away. You know, my grandmother lived here for something like forty years and she never learned to speak English fluently."

"Well, I sure hope I do better than your grandmother!" We both burst out laughing. "How does she manage to get along without speaking English?"

"Oh, she passed away. She's been dead for two years. She was very intelligent and could solve people's problems. My grandmother was the most wonderful person I ever met. We spoke in

Spanish all the time, just like you and me are doing right now. Abuelita used to even read to me in Spanish."

"You speak Spanish very well, Felita."

"Not as well as I used to. I know I make mistakes, but I like speaking it."

"You are Puerto Rican, right?"

"Right, born here. My parents are from the Island. I guess you can tell from my accent in Spanish." My accent in Spanish was different from his. Vinny spoke slowly and pronounced his words carefully, while us Puerto Ricans speak much faster.

"I noticed that most of the kids in school are Puerto Rican too, yet many don't speak Spanish as well as you do. Did you ever live in Puerto Rico, Felita?"

"No, I've never been there. But it's funny that you asked me that because guess what? I'm going to be spending the whole summer there. It will be my first visit. I can't wait!"

"That's wonderful! I wish I could speak English the way you speak Spanish, Felita. You know I really want to learn. And, frankly, that's why I came looking for you, to see if you could help me out. Can you help me, Felita? To speak English I mean?"

"What?" I couldn't believe he was asking me to help him.

"Look," he went on, "I'll be honest with you. I've been watching you and I see the way you work. You are a good student. You're always in the library, studying. And the way you draw is terrific. Those pictures that you have on display are great. See, I've been trying to talk to somebody, like one of the other students, but I just didn't know who to ask. Then I noticed you and watched

you and thought, all right, she's the one! Felita
is really smart and speaks Spanish, so I can talk
to her."

Vinny stopped and looked at me with a hurt
expression. "Some of the other students make fun
of me and call me names. I want to speak cor-
rectly. I don't want to stay speaking English the
way I do now. Will you help me, Felita?"

"Me—but how?" I couldn't imagine what I
could do to help.

"Teach me to speak English just like you and
the other kids do."

"You know, Vinny, they got extra classes in
school where foreign people learn English. I know
because some of my parents' friends from Puerto
Rico went there. Let me ask for you. Maybe they
might even give you special instructions because
you are a kid. Tomorrow I'll ask Mr. Richards—"

"No"—he cut me off—"I'm not interested
in learning any more grammar or English out of
books. I can do that myself. What I need is to talk
like any other kid. Not out of books, but just regular conversation. Will you help me, please?"

"I still don't know what I can do." I was
getting pretty confused.

"It's very simple. We can meet after school,
not each day, but perhaps two times a week. We
can just talk about anything. This way I can begin
to sound like everybody else."

"I really don't know about that." Vinny
stopped and stood before me, his pale green eyes
staring sadly at me.

"Please. Look, Felita, you say that you are
going to Puerto Rico this summer. And that your
Spanish isn't all that good, right? Well, what if I
help you out with Spanish? Wouldn't you like to

speak it better and learn to read and write it? In this way we can help each other out."

I thought about his offer and felt a rush of excitement going right through me. Imagine, out of all the kids in our school, it was going to be me teaching English to Vinny Davila, who all my girlfriends like and act silly around and drool over. The more I thought about it, the more it seemed almost too good to be true. And then I remembered my parents, especially Mami. How could I ever convince her I should have lessons with a boy? And worse yet, a stranger she'd never even met!

"Don't you think it's a good idea, Felita?"

"Sure I do. In fact I miss not being able to speak to my grandmother in Spanish, and I am going to Puerto Rico, so I would like to speak it as good as possible."

"So, do we have a deal?" I didn't know how to answer Vinny. I mean tackling Mami was a heavy order, and yet I didn't want to say no to this opportunity of having lessons with Vinny Davila.

"Let me talk to my mother and see what I can do." I could hardly believe what I'd just heard myself say.

"Wonderful! Thank you so much!" Vinny got so excited he spun around and clapped a few times.

"Hey, wait a minute, Vinny. I'm telling you right now I can't make any promises. I still have to figure out a few things and get permission."

"All right, but you will let me know soon?"

"I'll let you know when I know what's happening. We can talk in school in a free period or you can come to the library when I'm there, okay?"

"That's really great. Thank you so much." He paused and glanced at me, looking a little embarrassed. "There's just one more thing. I don't want the other kids in school to know about our lessons— at least not in the beginning. I'd like to wait until I'm speaking better in English. Can we keep this to ourselves?"

"Sure," I said. This was even better than I thought. The fact that Vinny Davila and me shared a secret made me feel special.

"I have to run or I'll be late." I turned and ran up the steps. "See you!" I called out to him in English.

"See you!" I heard his voice echoing me in English.

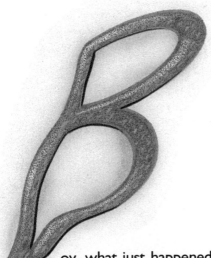

oy, what just happened, anyway? Here I had just agreed to have lessons with Vinny Davila. I couldn't believe it and inside my stomach it felt like butterflies were doing flip-flops. I couldn't get over the fact that he needed my help. At home I looked at myself in the mirror. I know he thinks I'm smart, but maybe he thinks I'm pretty too. I wished my eyes were bigger like Vivian's and that my nose was nice and straight like Consuela's instead of looking like a button on my face. Oh, well, I was glad Vinny liked my drawings. I had done two big drawings to celebrate Lincoln's and Washington's birthdays. I had copied the scenes from a magazine, but naturally I had added my own special touches so that they wouldn't be plain old copies. When I thought of the girls at school, especially Vivian, I got a case of the giggles. Wait till she hears that Vinny Davila, who she moans and groans over, has asked me to help him! Too much!

The more I thought about this whole business, the more anxious I got wondering how to work it out with Mami. I had to think very carefully now and plan things so that they would turn out just right. I had one lucky break—Papi was home. With him here I could at least argue my case. Getting my parents to listen without my brothers hearing us was next to impossible. In our small apartment there was always somebody in the living room or kitchen and everyone could hear what you said. I decided to bring it out in the open, and the best time would be tonight when everybody would be in a good mood because Papi was home.

t supper Mami and Papi were talking about the trip. I listened, waiting for the right moment.

"I already wrote to my sister Julia," Mami said, "and to my father. God, to think we have three children growing up without knowing their own family. Julia's boys are almost Tito and Johnny's ages, and my brother Tomás's boy and girl are a little younger than Felita. Imagine how happy my father is going to be. He keeps on saying in his letters that all he wants before he dies is to see his grandchildren."

"Rosa, that man is as healthy as an ox," said Papi. "Not many men outlive two wives and then get married for a third time at age seventy. He'll live a long time yet."

"I know. My father is something else all right! But it's going to be so good for all of us. This family reunion has been long overdue."

"I can't wait to meet my cousins," I said, thinking it was a good time to start, "but I wonder if they know how to speak English?"

"Felita"—Mami looked surprised—"you know that in Puerto Rico people speak Spanish. That's the language there."

"Well, Felita has a point," said Papi, "because they teach English in school. And anyway, what with all the traveling back and forth from the Island to here, I'm sure by now most people know some English."

"I sure hope so." I sighed.

"Felita, but you understand Spanish," said Tio Jorge, "and you also speak it pretty good. All them years talking to your grandmother must have taught you something."

"Yeah, but Abuelita's been dead for two years and I don't hardly speak it anymore."

"Your brothers are in the same situation, and they don't look worried to me. Do you, boys?" Papi looked at Johnny and Tito.

"I haven't even thought about it, Papi," said Johnny. "Besides, I understand almost everything, and I'm taking it in school. Remember?"

"I'm doing real good in Spanish. It's one of my best subjects," Tito said. "I'll make myself understood in P.R. No sweat."

"Felita, are you really worried?" Tio asked. I nodded. "Well, then we can speak in Spanish from now on. That should help you."

It's now or never, I thought. Go for it! "Something even better came up." Everybody stopped eating and looked at me. "You see, there's this new kid in our school. He just registered last month. He comes from Colombia in South America, you know." I told them about Vinny and his problem with learning English and how the kids make fun of him. "He got this idea that I could help him with his English and in exchange he could help me with my Spanish. Sort of a trade-off, you know." I paused and waited, but no one said anything. "I really think it's a great idea, especially since I'm going to Puerto Rico and it will help me when I have to talk Spanish there." My mother was speechless, then she looked at my father, who smiled and shrugged.

"Is that the boy that lives right here on our block?" Johnny asked me.

"Yeah, that's him. His name is Vinny Davila. He lives down the block, near the other corner from us, but across the street."

"Do you know him?" Papi asked Johnny.

"I've just seen him around, that's all. But he seems like a good kid. He always says hello when he sees me."

"I seen him too," said Tito. "You remember, Ma. We both seen the whole family. That time when we came from shopping last week, and you said they seem like nice people?"

"Oh, that's right." My mother nodded. "I remember now. But why can't this boy get extra help in English from the schools where there are teachers trained for that? Why do you have to give him lessons, Felita? Since when have you become an English teacher!"

"Because, Mami, he wants to learn conversation—how to talk regular English like the rest of us kids. He doesn't want an English teacher. That's the whole point! Teachers ain't going to be able to teach him like another kid can. Right, Johnny?"

"Maybe so." Johnny looked like he almost agreed.

"Well, I think Felita is right. There are certain things you ain't gonna get in school." When I heard Tito say this, I was almost shocked out of my chair.

My jaw just about dropped to the floor. Man, I don't remember the last time Tito had been on my side for anything!

"Sure you would say that"—Papi shook his head—"our number-one student here! Since when, Tito, are you an expert on school?"

"Aw, man, Papi," Tito spoke up, "come on, admit she's got a point. The kid wants to be accepted, to be like one of us. That's all. All the other kids will keep right on teasing him until he learns our ways. That's just the way it is, and he ain't gonna learn regular expressions and how to fit in with other kids from a teacher."

"Papi, Tito is right," I said. "And it wouldn't be no trouble, honest. We could meet like twice a week after school and spend an hour or so working on conversations. Me teaching him English and him teaching me Spanish."

"But why can't he learn from another boy?" I knew Mami would ask something like that. "There are plenty of boys in that school, chica. Why you?"

"Mami, first of all most of the boys make mean fun of him, real nasty fun, and second he asked me because I do speak Spanish. This way we can communicate. Plus here's the best part. He can really help me with my Spanish, which is pretty rusty by now. He even said he'll teach me to read and write in Spanish. It would really help me when I get to P.R. Remember, I'm going to have to be there for the whole summer with people who probably don't speak English." I waited and no one said anything. I stared at Papi, silently pleading my case.

"It can't do no harm, Rosa," said Papi.

"Where are these lessons going to take place, then, young lady?" asked Mami.

"We can meet here if you like, or in his house. Anywhere you say, Mami."

"I don't know, let me think about it." I knew I couldn't let her think about it even for one second. She had to agree before we all left the table.

"Aw, come on, Mami, it'll all be for a good cause. He can learn English and I can learn Spanish." I turned to my father. "Please, Papi! Come on, what's wrong with such a great idea?" Papi smiled, and I knew right then I had to get his okay.

"Look," I said, "we can try it and if you see anything wrong, anything at all, or if you don't like Vinny, we'll stop. Honest, I swear. What's bad about that?"

"It's okay with me if it's all right with your mother."

I turned toward my mother. "Mami? Say it's okay. Please, please!"

"Bueno...okay." My mother heaved a big sigh. "But we just try it, that's all, and then see how it goes. There is nothing definite, you understand?"

"Terrific. Thanks, Mami! Vinny will really be happy."

"And if you want to practice Spanish with me, you just let me know," said Tio Jorge.

"Thank you, I will, Tio."

"We'll look out for her, Mami," said Johnny. That really annoyed me. Nobody had asked for his two cents. But I thought I'd better leave things alone, since everything was going good. Tito, to my surprise, said nothing. I looked up at him, and when our eyes met, I silently thanked him.

Mami decided that Vinny and I would meet after school at four o'clock on Mondays and Thursdays and work for an hour. The lessons would be at my house. After a few weeks, if everything worked out okay between Vinny and me, we could talk about alternating one week at my house and one week at his house. But for now lessons were to be right in our living room, where Mami could watch us.

It was Thursday of the first week and we were up to our second lesson. As I was waiting for Vinny, I overheard Mami talking to Tio Jorge. "That boy has wonderful manners, Tio Jorge, and it's a pleasure talking with him. There is something about the way children are brought up in a Latino culture that is missing here. They are taught to respect their elders. Imagine, Vinny is only twelve and already he's un hombrecito.[3] I wish our Tito acted as well. That's why I'm glad we are all going to Puerto Rico and that Felita will be staying the whole summer. Maybe my kids will learn and see things the way we used to."

[3] a young man

"He's a good boy, Rosa," Tio Jorge agreed. "I'm going to invite him to look at my nature collection." When I heard that, I knew Tio Jorge liked Vinny, because he doesn't offer to show his collection to just anybody.

I had to admit that I was really beginning to like Vinny. And I mean a lot; like maybe more than friends. But I didn't want to become all gushy and dopey like the way my girlfriends acted with him at school. And besides, I didn't even know if he liked me—in that way, I mean. The whole idea made me so nervous that I decided I wasn't gonna think about it too much. I'd just concentrate real hard on our lessons and see what happened.

When Vinny came, he brought me two books in Spanish—a second grade reader and a book of children's stories with colorful pictures. I found that I could read and understand most of the children's stories, but with the reader there were a lot of words and phrases I didn't quite get. This weekend my brother Johnny was taking me to a bookstore where we could buy a Spanish/English dictionary. Tio Jorge had given me the money for it. He figured I should be well prepared in Spanish when I got to Puerto Rico.

When Vinny lived in Colombia, he had seen the Star Wars movies and really loved them. After I told him I had all the paperbacks—*Star Wars, The Empire Strikes Back,* and *Return of the Jedi*—he got real excited and asked if we could work with these books. I had dug them out and now I gave them to him. But he just nodded and looked upset.

"Hey, what's up? I thought you wanted these books," I said. Most of the time we still spoke in Spanish.

"I do, it's not that. In fact they're really great. It's something else." He sounded real serious.

"What else?"

"Felita, you gotta help me with a word that's not in the English dictionary."

"Sure. What is it?"

"It's called 'bimbo.'"

"Where did you hear that?" I started laughing, but he got so upset that I stopped.

"Joey Ramos and some of the other boys stopped me and told me I was going to have a new nickname. From now on, they said, they were calling me 'Bimbo Vinny.' They said it means being smart. But I figured they were lying and it probably means something else, something bad. Am I right?"

"You're right, Vinny, it doesn't mean smart. It means just the opposite—stupid or dummy."

"You see? I was right! I knew it just by the expressions on their faces and the way they were all laughing."

"What did you do?"

"Don't worry, I stood up to them and spoke to them in English. I said, 'No way! You don't call me this. Please to call me by my name. Vinny, understand? That is my only name, Vinny!'"

"You told them that? You said 'no way'?"

"Was that good, what I told them, Felita?"

"You did great! Vinny, you're learning fast. It just proves how smart you are and what a bunch of 'bimbos' they all are."

"Don't worry, Felita. When I get real good at speaking English, I'll tell them a lot more. Listen, I'm real happy to be taking these lessons with you."

After our lesson Mami walked in, acting real friendly, and asked us to come into the kitchen. She had set out two tall glasses of milk and two plates of her homemade bread pudding.

"You two have been working hard. I thought that before Vinny goes home he'd like a little bit of bread pudding. It's Puerto Rican style. I make it with brown sugar. I hope you like it, Vinny."

Mami makes the best bread pudding in the world. This was a treat all right. Usually we only got to eat it on Sundays. She asked him all about school and our lessons.

"Mrs. Maldonado, Felita is a fine teacher, and I am very grateful that you allow her to help me," he said.

"Well, you two just keep up the good work," she said. Now I knew she really liked him. When I walked Vinny to the door and we said good-bye, we exchanged glances, knowing we were both relieved that Mami approved of our lessons.

Celebrate

Our Differences

Who is the "average American teenager"? The young people who fill our schools in urban America and in many rural areas are not always white or middle class. They do not always live in a two-parent home with a backyard and a picket fence.

I know, because I was such a child who didn't fit into the stereotype of the average American girl. Growing up, I shared a crowded household with my parents, six older brothers, an aging aunt, and a cousin. We lived in an urban village, a *barrio,* nestled in the heart of New York City. The peo-ple in my neighborhood were mostly Puerto Ri-cans, and we shopped in the *bodegas,* ate plantains with rice and beans, lis-tened to the Spanish radio programs, and on Sunday attended the Spanish mass.

We also loved the com-ics: Dick Tracy and Bat-man and Robin. Along with my brothers, I sent in the top of cereal boxes with the required money and waited with happy an-ticipation for that special magic ring or a set of su-per, three-dimensional spy glasses. At home and within our community, I communicated in Spanish. That was my language of

Nicholasa Mohr at her eighth grade graduation

by Nicholasa Mohr

family, but English was our language of survival. We had to excel in school in order to get ahead and that meant learning English and reading well. When I was seven, my older brother Vincent took me to the library. Library card in hand, I took out my first book, Collodi's *Pinocchio*. I thought I would never again read such a wonderful book. But the librarian gave me *Grimm's Fairy Tales* and thus began my love affair with reading. However, when I searched for books that represented me and my family, I did not find them.

Storytelling held an important place in my up-bringing. As a child, when things became bleak at home, someone was sick, or the family faced a crisis, any one of the adults would tell us a story. As we listened, our spirits were lifted and we forgot our problems sharing in this magic gift of storytelling. Therefore, when I began to write, I told stories that came from my own background. Using my imagination, I re-created vital experiences and life within my Hispanic American culture that so far had been largely ignored and were not in our books or part of our literature.

What makes America special is that we are a diverse nation; we can share and celebrate our differences. Our culture, therefore, is always changing, offering new insights and challenging our ability to learn and grow. When I write about childhood memories and make stories, I also validate my heritage and celebrate my future. The young people who are now entering our nation from all around the world bring us their stories. I hope they too will write, make music, paint, or create films and share their unique experiences. For, in this way, America will ensure that it is a nation where all its children can claim their rightful place as Americans.

Thinking About it

1. Have you ever needed coaching in something as Vinny did—in a school subject or a sport, for example? How did you feel about asking for help? Did your experience work out as well as Vinny's?

2. The *tone* of a story is how the author feels about the characters, and it can include how the characters feel about each other. How would you describe the tone of this story? What parts of it would you read to show that tone?

3. You are going off to live in a country where no one speaks the language you know. Plan ahead! What are you going to do about it now and when you get there?

Song of the

Chirimia

Retold by Jane Anne Volkmer

On the night of the 20th full moon of Clear Sky's kingly reign, a child was born to him. Under the moon's bright light, he stood motionless, gazing at the baby girl in his servant's arms.

"I shall name my daughter Moonlight," Clear Sky declared, "to honor the light in which I first saw her." The child was all the king had now. His beloved queen had died at Moonlight's birth.

As Moonlight grew, Clear Sky's love for her deepened. Some days he would take her out in a boat on a nearby lake. They would watch the fishermen throw their nets into the clear blue waters. Patiently the two would wait until the men lifted the nets wriggling with fish.

Other days the two would walk through the marketplace to see the merchants' displays. Moonlight's eyes reflected the sun's sparkle on gold necklaces. Her voice had the softness and warmth of woven cloth.

As she talked gaily to Clear Sky, she danced past the displays, breathing the fragrance of cacao beans.

But one day, the happiness ended. Moonlight sat on the palace steps, staring at the ground, not caring what could be seen at the market or how many fish were netted. She would not talk to anyone, not even her father.

She wanted to be alone.

Her father tried to bring back her laughter and chatter.

He gave her glistening jade beads from the highlands. He had his hunters bring exotic birds to her from the jungle. He called the best ballplayers in the kingdom to play in the ball court before her. But Moonlight remained silent.

Clear Sky could not sleep.

He told his counselors, "My grieving will not end until I see a smile on Moonlight's face."

Clear Sky summoned governors, priests, and scribes to his chambers to ponder this problem of gloom. The learned men sat quietly for many hours, trying to think of a solution.

Finally, a scribe who recorded marriages in his village broke the silence. "Moonlight has become a young woman. It is the time of her life to marry. When she marries, her sorrow will leave."

"She shall be married!" proclaimed the king.

Clear Sky ordered all the young, unmarried men in the kingdom to come to the central plaza on the day of the 224th full moon of his rule. On this day, Moonlight could choose her husband.

As ordered, the suitors arrived at the palace on the day of the full moon. Many brought expensive gifts of jade, pottery, gold, and birds. Handsome men, strong men, knowledgeable men—all stood waiting. Each paraded before Moonlight in elegant clothing and spoke to her of his best qualities.

But she did not smile. She did not even listen.

As the sun lowered, the faint sounds of a song drifted through the crowd. On the path leading to the plaza, a man walked. He had no gifts. He carried no weapons. His clothes were not elegant. He

was singing a joyful song. The evening breeze captured his low, sweet voice and carried it to Moonlight's ears. Smiling, she lifted her head to hear the song better.

"Tell that young man to come into my chambers," the king commanded.

The dark-haired singer was brought before the king. He stood tall and slender before Clear Sky and Moonlight.

"What is your name?" Clear Sky asked.

"I am called Black Feather," he replied.

"Black Feather, you have brought pleasure to my daughter. If she wishes, you may marry her."

Moonlight smiled at Black Feather. "Your voice is clear and your song more pure than any I have ever heard," she said. "But I still prefer to listen to the harmony of singing birds. If you can make your song and your voice become one as the birds do, I shall marry you."

"I will learn to sing like the birds," he said, "but it will take me some time. Will you grant me time to learn?"

"How much time will you need?" she asked.

"Three full moons," he answered.

"I shall listen for your return."

With love in his heart, Black Feather left the king's chambers. He hurried down the palace steps. A large cluster of ceiba trees at the plaza's edge rustled for him to come to them. A small opening between the trees led to a path. This path would take him far into the woods, where it was said that the birds never stop singing.

Black Feather disappeared down the steep and narrow path. He walked through the darkness till he could go no farther. Black Feather lay on the ground and fell asleep.

At dawn, Black Feather woke to the sound of singing birds. He listened intently. Morning, noon, and evening, Black Feather tried his best to sing as sweetly as they did.

But he could not.

Two full moons passed, and Black Feather grew weary from trying.

Alone in the woods, Black Feather thought he would never be able to return to Moonlight. Suddenly, leaves started falling around him, and the wind blew cold and moist.

Startled, Black Feather looked up. Like a large tree bent in the wind, the Great Spirit of the Woods floated above him.

"Why do you look so sad?" whispered the Great Spirit.

With much dismay, Black Feather told the spirit his story.

"I know a way for your voice and your song to join in harmony so you can sing like a bird," crackled the Great Spirit. "But you must do as I tell you. First, cut a branch from that tree."

Black Feather took his knife and cut the branch. He handed it to the Great Spirit.

Howling, the spirit flew into a treetop, setting it ablaze. The spirit roared and hissed as he transformed the branch into a long, hollow pipe with holes in one side.

The flames vanished, and the spirit drifted slowly back to Black Feather.

The Great Spirit gave the pipe to the young man saying, "What you hold in your hands is called a chirimia, and its song is more pleasing to the ear than that of the birds. Learn to play it well, and when the princess hears the chirimia's song, she will marry you."

Black Feather stared at the pipe.

"Take it to your lips and blow through it," the spirit commanded. "Move your fingers along the holes and listen."

Then the Great Spirit swirled into a spiral of blue-gray smoke and disappeared into the pipe.

Black Feather put his lips to the chirimia and blew. A remarkable sound filled the air, a sound so melodious that even the birds stopped their singing.

Black Feather practiced playing on the pipe all day long. The sounds became clearer and purer with every note he played.

Many days passed, and the time came for Black Feather to return. As he walked swiftly through the woods, Black Feather held tightly onto the pipe.

When he neared the small opening in the ceiba trees, he put the chirimia to his lips and began to play a song from his heart.

The melody brought the princess out of the palace to listen. Her eyes fell upon Black Feather, and she exclaimed, "Your song is lovelier than those of the birds!"

On that night, the 227th full moon of Clear Sky's reign, Moonlight and Black Feather married. Under the moon's bright light, Clear Sky stood motionless, listening to the song of the chirimia while Moonlight danced in the plaza below.

Today, if you travel to Guatemala, you may hear music sweeter than that of any bird, lilting in the wind. If you ask what it is you hear, the reply will be, "It is the song of the chirimia, the most harmonious song in the woods."

Thinking About It

1. This story has lasted two thousand years. Some would say that it speaks across the ages. What is its appeal? Why will people still read it or listen to it?

2. After the wedding, Black Feather granted an interview about his journey and how he achieved his goal. Now you tell it for him. What did he do for himself? What did others do for him?

3. If this story were told about today's times, would the music be different? Would the source of the music be different? What would you put into a modern version of this folk tale?

Another Book About a Quest

The House in the Woods by Isabelle Holland is a modern-day quest. Bridget searches for a solution to her problems. She believes her adoptive father hates her, and she feels guilty about not being able to help her brother Morgan. Then she and Morgan find an old house in the woods that seems to hold some secret. Will it help Bridget find answers and happiness?

The Arrow and the Lamp

Retold by Margaret Hodges

On the Greek island of Rhodes is "the valley of the butterflies." Every summer, countless thousands of butterflies settle there on the leaves of the trees. When they are disturbed, they fly up in a golden cloud, and the Greeks say that each butterfly is a soul, like Psyche. This is her story.

The Characters in the Story

Psyche (Sī′kē) meaning the Mind, the Soul, or the Self.

Aphrodite (Af ro dī′tē) called Venus in Roman myth; she is the goddess of love and beauty.

Eros (E′ros) called Amor or Cupid in Roman myth; he is the son of Aphrodite and makes both gods and humans fall in love.

Persephone (Per sef′o nē) called Proserpina in Roman myth; with Hades (Hā′dēs), her husband, she rules over the underground world of the dead, also called Hades, which is reached by crossing the river Styx (Stix). King Hades is Pluto in Roman myth.

Zeus (Zūs) called Jupiter or Jove in Roman myth; he is "the father of light" and ruler of the gods, all of whom live on Mount Olympus. They drink nectar and eat ambrosia, which makes them immortal.

Once a king and a queen had three daughters. All three were beautiful, but the youngest, Psyche, was different. Her sisters were content to know what they were told. Psyche always wanted to know more. She was so lovely that men called her a new Aphrodite, a young goddess of love and beauty, but no man dared to marry a goddess. So while the two older sisters found husbands and went away to live in their own homes, Psyche stayed on alone with her father and mother.

Now all might have been well if golden, sweet-smiling Aphrodite had not heard of Psyche. The goddess came up out of the sea to find out whether men were really leaving her temples empty and silent and throwing flowers in the streets where Psyche walked. And when Aphrodite saw that it was true, she no longer smiled. She was furious, and she said to herself, "This girl is mortal. Beautiful she may be, but like all mortals she will die, and until she dies, she must never have a happy day. I shall see to that."

Then she called her favorite child, Eros, and he came flying to her. This young god, as fair as his mother, had golden wings on which he moved swiftly and unseen on his mysterious errands, often doing mischief. He carried a golden bow and a quiver filled with arrows.

"Go to this girl, this Psyche," said Aphrodite. "Wound her with one of your arrows. Pour bitterness on her lips. Then find her the vilest husband in the world—mean, bad-tempered, ugly—and make her fall in love with him."

There were two springs of water in Aphrodite's garden—one bitter, the other sweet. Carrying water from both springs, Eros flew off, invisible.

He found Psyche asleep. Her beauty moved him to pity, but, obeying his mother's command, he poured bitter water on her lips and touched her side with one of his arrows. Psyche felt the pain and opened her eyes. She could not see Eros, but as he looked into her eyes, the arrow trembled in his hand, and by chance he wounded himself. He poured a little of the sweet water on her forehead, and flew away.

Still no lovers came to ask for Psyche's hand in marriage, so the king and the queen, guessing that their daughter had somehow angered one of the gods, asked an oracle to look into the future and tell them what could be done to find a husband for her.

The oracle answered with frightening words: "Dress your daughter for her funeral. She will never marry a mortal man but will be the bride of a creature with wings, feared even by the gods. Take Psyche to the stony top of the mountain that looks down on your city, and leave her there alone to meet her fate."

When they heard this prophecy, all the people wept with Psyche's father and mother. But Psyche said, "Tears will not help me. I was doomed from the moment when you called me the new Aphrodite. It must be Aphrodite herself whom I have angered. Obey the oracle before the goddess punishes all of you. I alone must bear her anger."

Psyche led the way to the mountaintop and said good-bye to her weeping parents and the crowd of folk who had sadly followed her. When all were gone, she sat down, trembling and afraid, to wait. But no monster husband came. Instead, the warm west wind began to blow and, raising her gently in the air, carried her down the far side of the mountain to a green and flowering meadow in a hidden valley.

Psyche fell peacefully asleep in the soft grass. When she woke, she saw a grove of tall trees watered by a clear stream. In the grove stood a marvelous palace, its golden pillars topped with a roof of carved sandalwood and ivory.

She entered through the open doorway, wondering at the light that flashed from silver walls. Surely only a god could have made such a palace! Psyche passed from room to room, walking on floors made of precious stones, until she came to a marble pool filled with scented water.

Then a voice spoke to her: "Lady, all of this is yours. Ask for whatever you like." Unseen hands led her to the bath and afterward clothed her in a robe of fine silk. A table appeared, spread with delicious food, and Psyche ate and drank while invisible servants waited on her and the air was filled with the sound of sweet voices singing.

When darkness fell, Psyche found a bed ready for her and lay down to rest. But in the night she woke, feeling the presence of someone standing beside her bed, and she was full of fear. Then a voice said, "Do not be afraid, Psyche. I am the husband you have been waiting for. Trust me. No harm will come to you. Only do not try to see me." Psyche's husband stayed with her all night long, but before daylight he was gone.

For some months Psyche lived in the palace, surrounded by beauty and comfort. The unseen servants answered all her wishes and when her unseen husband came at night, he was always kind. She began to long for the sound of his voice and very soon fell deeply in love with him. Still, the days seemed empty and she often felt lonely.

One night her husband said to her, "Psyche, your sisters are looking for you. If you hear them calling, do not answer."

Psyche promised to obey, but she wished more and more to see a face. The clear waters of the pool reflected only her own face, and the palace now seemed like a prison. At last her husband found her weeping and, taking her in his arms, said, "Well, my love, have your wish, even if it brings trouble. The west wind shall carry your sisters here." And Psyche thanked him with grateful kisses.

The next day she heard her sisters calling to her from the mountaintop, and she called back to them. Then the west wind carried them down into the valley, and when they found Psyche safe and well, they embraced her joyfully. But their joy turned to jealousy as she showed them her palace and they saw how she was dressed and waited on like a queen.

When Psyche confessed that she had never seen her husband, they spoiled her happiness by planting suspicions in her mind: "If your husband will not let you see him, he must be the monster that the oracle said you would marry. He is only biding his time until he is ready to kill you. Take our advice. The next time he comes, have a lamp and a sharp knife hidden at your side. When he is asleep, light the lamp and look at him. If he is a monster, kill him while there is yet time."

The west wind carried the sisters away as safely as they had come, but Psyche was tormented by what they had said. At last she filled a little lamp with oil and found a sharp knife, both of which she hid beside her bed.

That night, when her husband was asleep, she lit the lamp and saw him—not a monster, but the most beautiful of beings, a fair and graceful youth with golden wings, smiling even in his sleep. Psyche was moved by a deeper love than she had ever felt. She bent over her husband, and from the lamp, a drop of oil, burning hot, fell on his shoulder. Stung by the pain, he opened his eyes and looked at her sternly. "Foolish Psyche," he said, "I knew how it would be. You could not trust me. You had to see for yourself. Now you will lose everything that I could give you, and I must lose you." Too late she knew who he was: Eros, the son of Aphrodite. There was a flash of golden wings and he was gone. The palace too was gone, and Psyche found herself alone again on the mountaintop.

Psyche was determined to find her lost husband, but although she walked all the roads of the world, she could not discover where he was. He had flown to one of his mother's many palaces, sick at heart and feverish with the burning pain of the oil from Psyche's lamp. Aphrodite was angrier than she had ever been. "You are meant to make mortals fall in love, not to fall in love yourself," she said. "However, you will soon be well and will forget all about that girl." She locked him into a chamber, and there he lay.

As Psyche searched for Eros, she came at last to a faraway river that flowed from a high waterfall. At the edge of the river stood a temple, and in its doorway she saw Aphrodite. She knelt at the feet of the goddess and begged Aphrodite to tell her where she could find Eros. But Aphrodite, jealous of her beauty, answered with a false smile, "I will give Eros back to you if you will do some-

thing for me." And when Psyche eagerly agreed, the goddess led her into the temple and showed her a room filled with a great heap of grains: corn and barley, poppy seed, lentils, and beans, all mixed together. "Anyone as ugly as you is fit only to work," Aphrodite said, scornfully. "Sort all of these grains into separate piles, and have it done by evening."

When the goddess had left her, Psyche sat down and began to cry. The task was impossible. But as she sat there weeping, she saw a procession of little ants coming out of the earth and running to her rescue. They attacked the heap of grains and carried each kind to a separate pile, never stopping until the work was done. Then they vanished into the earth.

When Aphrodite returned in the evening, she found Psyche sitting with folded hands. All the work was finished. "You do not deceive me, wretched girl," cried the goddess. "Someone has helped you. Tomorrow you must work alone, but your task is easy. Across the river is a field where golden sheep are grazing. Bring me a strand of their fleece."

At dawn Psyche went to the river and stepped into the water. But as she did so, she heard the whispering of the reeds that grew along the shore: "Psyche, the sheep are wild rams, as fierce as the sun's rays. They will batter you with their stony foreheads and pierce you with their sharp horns."

Psyche was ready to sink down into the river, despairing. But the reeds whispered, "Do not give up. Be patient. Things will change. Wait until the sun sinks. Then the rams sleep, and you can easily gather a strand of their golden fleece from the bushes along the edge of the field." Psyche obeyed, and in the evening gave the shining fleece to Aphrodite.

The goddess was enraged. She could not bear to find Psyche still alive. "Tomorrow you must work again," she said. She gave Psyche a crystal jar and pointed to the waterfall that plunged from the mountain peak. "That is where the river Styx comes from Hades, the land of death. Bring me water from the top of the waterfall," she ordered. She thought to herself, "The girl will never return. It is a just punishment for stealing my son's love."

Psyche made her way to the foot of the mountain and climbed the steep and rugged path—up, up, on and on, fearing every moment that she would fall and be dashed to pieces. At last she reached the topmost crag, a rough and slippery rock, and saw that the torrent of water poured out of a cavern guarded by dragons with unwinking eyes. Psyche heard the waters roaring, "Beware!" and stood as if turned to stone by fear. Then, from high in the air above her, there flew down an eagle, the messenger of Zeus, king of the gods. The eagle took the crystal jar in its claws and swooped past the dragons. It hovered at the top of the waterfall until the jar was filled to the brim, then brought it back to Psyche.

That night Aphrodite could hardly believe her eyes when she saw Psyche alive and well, bearing the jar of water in her hands. "I have obeyed all your commands," said Psyche. "I beg you to give me my husband."

"I have only one more task for you," said Aphrodite with a bitter smile. "If you accomplish this, Eros shall be yours forever. Go to the world of the dead and ask Queen Persephone to fill this box with some of her beauty." "For," she thought to herself, "no mortal comes back from Hades."

Psyche took the box. She knew now that Aphrodite wished nothing less than her death, and she climbed a high tower, ready to leap to the ground and so be taken at once to the land of the dead, never to return. But as she looked out from the top of the windy tower, a voice echoed from its walls: "Psyche, do not lose hope. There is a way to accomplish the last of your labors. Near at hand you will find a cave. A path leads through it to the river Styx. Carry two coins in your mouth to pay the ferryman who will row you across the river to Hades and back again. A three-headed dog guards the palace of Hades. Take two barley cakes for the dog. Give him one when you enter, the other when you leave."

Psyche found the cave and followed the dark path that led through it into the secret places of the earth. When she came to the river Styx, the ferryman took one of the coins from her mouth and rowed her across. When the fierce three-headed dog of Hades barked at her, she silenced him with a barley cake and went on to the jeweled palace of Hades. There Queen Persephone came to greet her. And when Psyche saw that gentle face, she knew why even Aphrodite wanted to have some of its beauty. The goddess took the box and put something into it, saying in a voice both soft and kind, "Do not open this, my child. It is not for you."

Gratefully, Psyche took the box and ran from the palace. She gave her last cake to the three-headed dog, her last coin to the ferryman, and hurried up the path. But as she stepped out under the open sky, she thought, "My husband once said that I was beautiful. He may no longer think so, after all my labors. Perhaps I should keep a little of Persephone's beauty for myself." She opened the box. At once a deep sleep came over her, and she lay as if dead.

But even from afar, Eros saw her. He had recovered from his hurt, and his love for her was so strong that he burst open the locked door of his chamber and flew to her, tenderly wiping away the spell of sleep. He closed the box and gave it back to her. Then, with Psyche in his arms, he flew upward. As they neared the top of Mount Olympus the heavenly radiance shone brighter and brighter and in the center of the light Psyche saw Zeus, the father of light. He called Aphrodite and all the other gods and goddesses together and spoke to them: "See this mortal girl whom Eros loves. No mortal can have Persephone's beauty, but Psyche has brought some of that beauty to us. So give her the food and drink of gods, and let her be one of us, never to die, never to be separated again from her love."

Finally, even Aphrodite said it should be so. Then from Psyche's shoulders delicate wings, like those of a butterfly, unfolded. And mortals, seeing butterflies in summer fields, remember Psyche and her love.

Margaret Hodges
as a teenager

T h e Land of Mount Olympus

Margaret Hodges

by Margaret Hodges

The Arrow and the Lamp: the Story of Psyche is a Greek myth. Some people say that myths are not true because they are "only stories." But myths are full of truth because they tell us about ourselves. *The Arrow and the Lamp* shows how mysteriously love comes to us, how easily it can be lost, and what it may cost to win true love that lasts forever.

I was in the eighth grade when I first read the story of Psyche in a school textbook, Gayley's *Classic Myths*. I never forgot it, because it seemed to be about me and people I knew. I was not the most beautiful or the brightest girl in the world, but I liked to imagine that I was.

If you were the best-looking person in the world, would you be perfectly happy? Perhaps not; other people would be jealous of you. Would you be perfectly happy if you were the most intelligent person in the world? What if you could find no one who was your equal? Suppose you find a husband or wife after all, but he or she comes only in the dark of night and forbids you to try to see him or her. This is a story of suspense and danger and adventure from start to finish. And it ends on Mount Olympus, the home of the gods, where Eros took Psyche to live happily ever after.

My husband, too, read this wonderful story when he was in the eighth grade. Fifty years later, when our children were grown and gone from home, we began to travel, and our first trip abroad took us to Greece, the land of our young dreams, the land of Mount Olympus, home of the gods. One day, traveling by bus through the Greek mountains, we saw in our guidebook that we would pass Mount Olympus. The driver heard our excited voices and not long afterward stopped the bus. "Mount Olympus!" he called out with a broad smile for his American passengers.

Imagine it all for yourself, as we did long ago. The land of myth is still there.

Thinking About It

1. Did Psyche cause the things that happened to her, or was she the victim? What would she say? What would *you* say?

2. One reason that myths live thousands of years is that they have rich imagery—that is, they have glorious scenery and strange, exotic characters. Use the illustrations and the text of the Psyche myth to show the rich imagery that has helped keep this story alive.

3. You have read Psyche's story. Now think of other ways it could be told. How could the imagery be placed before a modern audience? Describe one way other than reading that the story could be told.

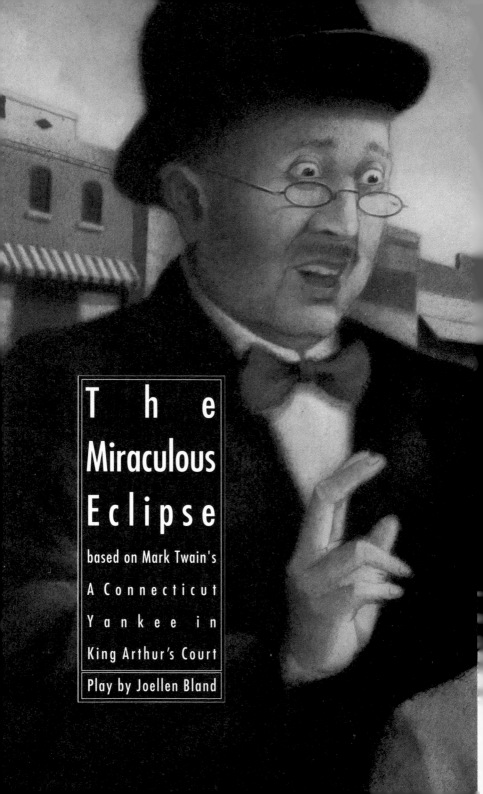

The Miraculous Eclipse

based on Mark Twain's

A Connecticut

Yankee in

King Arthur's Court

Play by Joellen Bland

CHARACTERS

Old Hank Morgan	**Merlin the Magician**
Boy	**Four Guards**
Hank Morgan,	**Courtiers,**
a young man	*lords and ladies*
Sir Kay,	**Knights**
knight of the Round Table	**Servants**
Clarence, *page*	**Herald**
King Arthur	

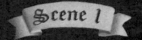

Scene 1

TIME: *1879.*

SETTING: *A street in Hartford, Connecticut. A barrel stands center.*

BEFORE RISE: OLD HANK MORGAN *enters slowly right, followed by BOY.*

BOY: Excuse me, Mr. Morgan.

OLD HANK *(Stopping and turning):* Yes?

BOY: Some of the boys have been telling me that . . . well, that you sure can tell a whale of a story!

OLD HANK: That's what they told you, is it? *(Fumbles in coat pockets, pulls out pipe)* You're new in town, aren't you?

BOY: Yes, sir. The boys dared me to ask you to tell *your* version of the story of King Arthur and his knights of the Round Table.

OLD HANK: They did, eh? Well, son, it just so happens I knew King Arthur well when I was a young man, so I can tell you anything you want to know about him.

BOY *(Amazed):* You knew King Arthur?

OLD HANK *(Nodding):* I knew all the folks at Camelot, including that cagey old humbug, Merlin.

BOY *(In awe):* You knew Merlin the Magician? But they all lived in the sixth century!

OLD HANK *(Tamping his pipe):* That's right. And if it weren't for Merlin, I might still be in the sixth century myself! *(Smiles)* You don't believe me, do you?

BOY: Well, sir, if you've got some time, I'd like to hear your story. Then I'll tell you if I believe you.

OLD HANK: I've got all the time in the world. *(Sits on barrel and hunts through his pockets as he talks, finally coming up with tobacco pouch. BOY sits cross-legged on ground.)* You see, I was born and brought up right here in Hartford, Connecticut, so I am a Yankee of the Yankees, and very practical.

BOY: That's what the boys said about you, Mr. Morgan.

OLD HANK: As a young man, I first went to work as a blacksmith. Then later I went over to the Colt Arms Factory and learned how to make guns, cannons, boilers, engines—all sorts of labor-saving machinery. If there wasn't a quick, new-fangled way to make a thing, I'd invent one. I became head supervisor and had a couple of thousand men under me.

BOY *(Impressed):* A couple of thousand? Whew!

OLD HANK: Some of them were pretty rough characters, too. *(Stands)* Say, you just come on home with me and we'll sit on my front porch. It'll be more comfortable. (*Starts left.* BOY *follows, carrying barrel.*) I was a man full of fight when I was supervisor, but one day I met my match. A big fellow named Hercules and I had a misunderstanding, and we went after each other with crowbars.

BOY: That must have been some fight!

OLD HANK: It was! Hercules knocked me down with a crusher to my head that made everything crack! My world just went out in total darkness, and when I came to, I wasn't at the arms factory any more. (OLD HANK *and* BOY *exit left. Lights dim to indicate shift of scene to a country road in England. Lights come up full again on* HANK MORGAN *as a young man. He holds his head in pain.*)

YOUNG HANK: Oh, my aching head! Hercules will pay for this, or my name isn't Hank Morgan! (*Looks around*) Where am I? This doesn't look like any place I've seen around Hartford. (SIR KAY, *wearing full armor, bounds in left with sword drawn and takes threatening position in front of* HANK.)

SIR KAY: Will you joust, fair sir?

HANK (*Staring rudely*): Will I what?

SIR KAY (*Waving sword*): Will you fight with me to win land or lady or—

HANK (*Interrupting*): Now look here, who do you think you are, wearing that outlandish getup and swinging that dangerous weapon around? Get along back to the circus where you belong, or I'll report you!

SIR KAY (*Holding swordpoint to* HANK's *chest*): My name is Sir Kay, and in the name of the King, I take you captive! You are now my property and must come with me at once!

HANK *(Aside):* If this fellow isn't part of a circus, he must be crazy. But I'd better play along with him, or he might get nasty with that sword. *(Raises his hands in surrender and turns back to SIR KAY)* All right, Sir Kay, you've got me. Where to?

SIR KAY: This way! *(Starts off left, pushing HANK in front of him with sword)*

HANK: Uh, by the way, Sir Kay, how far are we from Hartford?

SIR KAY *(Puzzled):* I have never heard of that place.

HANK *(Stopping):* Never heard of Hartford? *(Aside)* I reckon he must be from out of state. *(Turns back to SIR KAY)* Well, what town are we headed for? Bridgeport?

SIR KAY *(Shaking his head):* Camelot! *(Pushes HANK forward)*

HANK: Camelot? There isn't any town by that name in Connecticut!

SIR KAY: You are not in Connecticut.

HANK *(Stopping again):* Well, where in the world am I?

SIR KAY: England! *(HANK's mouth drops open in astonishment, as SIR KAY pushes him off left.)*

TIME: *England, in the year 528.*

SETTING: *A courtyard in Camelot. At center is a throne on platform.*

AT RISE: COURTIERS, KNIGHTS, GUARDS *and* SERVANTS *move busily back and forth.* SIR KAY *and* HANK *enter left. At the sight of* HANK, *all stop to stare and point at him.*

COURTIERS *(Ad lib):* Look there! Did you

ever see anything like it? Look at his strange clothes! Be careful, don't get too close! (*Etc.*)

SIR KAY (*Poking HANK with sword*): I warn you, don't try to escape. (HANK *looks around, puzzled, as* CLARENCE *enters, smiling and looking HANK over from head to foot.*) My page, Clarence (*Pointing to him*), will keep you in charge until I come back for you. (*Exits right*)

HANK: Page, did he say? Go on! A boy your size can't be much more than a paragraph!

CLARENCE: You have an unusual way of speaking, sir, but you are welcome! I hope you will find me to be your true friend.

HANK: Well, my boy, if you're really my friend, you can tell me where I am. That escapee from a circus who brought me here said this was England, but he's obviously not in his right mind.

CLARENCE: Nay, sir, my master, Sir Kay, spoke the truth. You are in England.

HANK: England. (*Shakes his head*) Well, either I'm crazy or something just as awful has happened. Now tell me, honest and true, what is this place?

CLARENCE: Camelot, the court of King Arthur.

HANK: The King Arthur who had the Round Table?

CLARENCE: Is there any other, sir?

HANK (*Hesitantly*): And according to your notions, what year is it?

CLARENCE: The nineteenth of June, in the year five hundred twenty-eight.

HANK (*Repeating words mechanically*): Five twenty-eight? (*Turns away; in a daze*) Five twenty-eight. (*Looks at* COURTIERS, *then at himself*) I'm sure it was 1879 when I got up this morning. *I* look like 1879, but all these people look like . . . five twenty-eight. (*Pacing*) Five twenty-eight . . . that was the year when a total eclipse of the sun occurred . . . on June 21st at three minutes past noon. Just two days from now. (*Suddenly*) I've got an idea! If I can just keep hold of my senses for forty-eight hours, I'll know for certain if this boy is telling me the truth. (*Turns back to* CLARENCE) Tell me, Clarence, who is this Sir Kay?

CLARENCE: A brave knight, sir, and foster brother to our liege the King. You are his prisoner, and as soon as dinner is finished, he will exhibit you before the King and brag about capturing you. He'll exaggerate the facts a little, but it won't be safe to correct him. Then you'll be flung into a dungeon.

HANK (*Horrified*): Flung into a dungeon? What for?

CLARENCE (*Casually*): It is the custom. But never fear, I'll find a way to come and see you, and I'll help you get word to your friends who will come and ransom you.

HANK: Well, I'm much obliged to you, Clarence, but you see, all my friends won't even be born for more than thirteen hundred years. (*Fanfare of trumpets is heard off right.*)

CLARENCE: King Arthur is coming now. (HERALD *enters right, holding trumpet, and walks center.*)

HERALD: His Royal Majesty, King Arthur! (KING ARTHUR *enters, followed by* MERLIN, *and attended by several* KNIGHTS. *He sits on throne center.* COURTIERS *bow low and stand* *in groups at either side of throne.* SIR KAY *enters right, seizes* HANK *by arm and pushes him to his knees in front of* KING ARTHUR.)

SIR KAY *(Bowing low):* My lord King, most noble knights and ladies of the realm! Behold this curious captive I have conquered!

KING ARTHUR: And where did you find this strange creature, Sir Kay?

SIR KAY: I came upon this horrible ogre, my liege, in a far land of barbarians called Connecticut. Everyone there wears the same ridiculous clothing that he does, but I warn you, do not touch him! His clothing is enchanted! (COURTIERS *gasp and step back.*) It is intended to secure him from harm, but I overpowered the enchantment through my strong will and great courage! I killed his thirteen attending knights in a three hours' battle and took him prisoner!

HANK *(Starting to rise):* Now, just a minute—

SIR KAY *(Pushing* HANK *down):* Behold this enchanted, man-devouring monster who tried to escape from me by leaping into the top of a tree at a single bound!

HANK *(Starting up again):* Now, look here, you're carrying this thing a little too far—

SIR KAY *(Pushing him down roughly):* Behold this menacing barbarian while you may, good people, for at noon on the twenty-first he shall die!

HANK *(Jumping up):* What? What have I done to deserve death? I haven't even been in this century more than half an hour!

SIR KAY: You have suffered defeat at my hands, and I decide if you live or die. You must die!

KING ARTHUR: Well done, Sir Kay. But if his clothing is enchanted, how do you propose to put him to death? (COURTIERS *murmur excitedly.*)

SIR KAY: Surely Your Majesty's mighty magician, Merlin, can break the enchantment.

COURTIERS *(Ad lib):* Yes, yes! Merlin will know what to do! Try, Merlin! *(Etc.)*

MERLIN: Make way, please. (*He steps forward, makes several sweeping passes with his arms.* COURTIERS *fall back respectfully, and watch him intently.*) How can all of you be so dull? Has it not occurred to anyone here but me that the thing to do is to remove the enchanted clothing from this—(*In disgust*) this creature, and thus make him helpless and harmless? Proceed.

HANK *(Starting to back away):* Now, hold on here. . . . Hey! (FOUR GUARDS *seize* HANK, *push him to floor, pull off his boots, stockings, overalls, sweater, etc., leaving him wearing only his suit of long underwear.*)

MERLIN *(With a wicked laugh):* Now he is powerless!

SIR KAY: To the dungeon with him!

KING ARTHUR: A cheer for Sir Kay, truly a brave knight of the Table Round! (HANK *is dragged out left by* GUARDS, *as* COURTIERS *cheer* SIR KAY. *Curtain*)

Scene 2

SETTING: *Dungeon cell. Pile of straw and low stool are center. May be played before curtain.*

AT RISE: CLARENCE *sits on stool, watching* HANK, *who lies sleeping on straw.* HANK *stirs, stretches, his eyes still closed.*

HANK (*Not seeing* CLARENCE): What an astonishing dream I've just had! King Arthur's Court! What nonsense! (*Yawns and stretches*) I reckon the noon whistle will blow shortly, and then I'll go down to the factory and have it out with Hercules. (*Turns over, opens his eyes sleepily, sees* CLARENCE, *and sits up abruptly*) What! Are you still here? Go away with the rest of the dream! Scat!

CLARENCE (*Laughing*): Dream? What dream? (*Stands up*)

HANK: Why, the dream that I'm in the court of a king who never existed, and that I'm talking to you who are nothing but a work of my imagination!

CLARENCE (*Sarcastically*): Indeed! And is it a dream that you're going to be burned tomorrow?

HANK: Burned! (*Jumps up*) I'm still in the dungeon! This dream is more serious than I thought. (*Pleading*) Clarence, my boy, you're the only friend I've got. Help me think of a way to escape from this place.

CLARENCE: Escape? Why, the corridors are guarded by at least twenty men at arms. You cannot hope to escape. Besides . . . (*Hesitantly*) . . . there are other obstacles more overpowering than men at arms.

HANK: What are they?

CLARENCE (*Nervously*): Oh, I dare not tell you!

HANK: But you must! Come, be brave! Speak out!

CLARENCE (*Looking around fearfully, then speaking close to* HANK's *ear*): Merlin, that terrible and mighty magician, has woven wicked spells about this dungeon. No man can escape it and live! (*Nervously*) There, I have told you. Now be merciful, and do not betray me, or I am lost!

HANK (*Laughing*): Merlin has cast a few spells, has he? That cheap old humbug? Bosh!

CLARENCE (*Falling to his knees in terror*): Oh, beware of what you say! These walls may crumble on us at any moment. Call back your awful words before it is too late!

HANK (*Turning away; to himself*): If everyone here is as afraid of Merlin's pretended magic as Clarence is, certainly a superior man like me with my nineteenth-century education ought to be shrewd enough to take advantage of this situation. (*Thinks a moment, then turns back to* CLARENCE) Come on, Clarence, get up and pull yourself together. (CLARENCE *stands.*) Do you know why I laughed at Merlin?

CLARENCE (*Timidly*): No, and I pray you won't do it again.

HANK: I laughed because I'm a magician myself.

CLARENCE (*Recoiling*): You?

HANK: I've known Merlin for seven hundred years, and—

CLARENCE: Seven hundred years?

HANK: Don't interrupt! He has died and come alive again thirteen times. I knew him in Egypt three hundred years ago, and in India over five hundred years ago. He's always getting in my way everywhere I go, but his magic doesn't amount to shucks compared to mine. Now, look here, Clarence, I'll be your friend, and you must be mine.

CLARENCE: I *am* your friend, I assure you!

HANK: Good. Now, you get word to the King that I am the world's mightiest and grandest magician, and that if any harm comes to me I will quietly arrange a little calamity that will make the fur fly in these realms.

CLARENCE *(Terrified):* Yes, yes, at once!

(Backs off right, then turns and runs out)

HANK: That should get me off the hook pretty quick. *(Struts back and forth confidently for a moment, then suddenly stops)* Ah! What a blunder I've made! I sent Clarence off to alarm the King with the threat of a calamity I haven't thought of yet! These sixth-century people are childish and superstitious. They believe in miracles. Suppose they want to see a sample of my powers? Suppose the King asks me to name my calamity? (HANK *sinks down onto stool, chin in hands, as lights fade out. In a moment, lights come up again.* HANK *remains on stool in same position.)* I've got to stall for time. I can't think of anything. *(Looks off right)* Here's Clarence. I have to look confident. (CLARENCE *enters right, dejectedly.)* Well?

CLARENCE: I took your message to my liege the King, and he was very much afraid. He was ready to order your release, but Merlin was there and spoiled everything.

HANK: I might have known.

CLARENCE: He persuaded the King that you are crazy, and that your threat is nothing but foolishness because you have not named your calamity. Oh, my friend, be wise and name it, or you may still be doomed! (HANK, *deep in thought, frowns, then suddenly smiles.*)

HANK: Ah! I have it! Just in time, too. (*Turns to CLARENCE and draws himself up haughtily*) How long have I been shut up in this miserable hole?

CLARENCE: Since yesterday evening.

HANK: Then today is the twentieth of June?

CLARENCE: Yes.

HANK: At what time tomorrow am I to be burned?

CLARENCE (*Shuddering*): At high noon.

HANK: Listen carefully. I will tell you what to say to the King. (*In deep, measured tones*) Tell him that at high noon tomorrow I will smother the entire world in the dead blackness of midnight!

CLARENCE (*Falling to his knees*): Oh, have mercy!

HANK (*Dramatically*): I will blot out the sun, and it will never shine again! The fruits of the earth shall rot for lack of light, and the people of the earth shall famish and die to the last man! Go! Tell the King! (CLARENCE *staggers to his feet and backs off right, in terror.*)

HANK (*Slapping his knee*): Ha! The eclipse will be sure to save me, and make me the greatest man in the kingdom besides! Furthermore, I'll be the boss of the whole country within three months. After all, I have thirteen hundred years' head start on the best-educated man in the kingdom! (*Sits down, smiling, then suddenly frowns*) Hm-m, I hope my threat won't be too much for these simple people. Suppose they want to compromise? Then what do I do? (*Lights fade out for a moment to indicate brief* *passage of time, then come up again.* HANK *remains seated.*) Of course, if they want to compromise, I'll listen, but I'll have to stand my ground and play my hand for all it's worth. (1ST *and* 2ND GUARDS *enter right.*)

1ST GUARD: Come! The stake is ready!

HANK *(Terrified):* The stake! (GUARDS *seize him.*) But . . . but . . . wait a minute! The execution is tomorrow!

2ND GUARD: The order has been changed and set forward a day. Come! (GUARDS *drag* HANK, *speechless, out right. Curtain*)

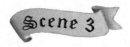

Scene 3

SETTING: *Courtyard in Camelot. There is a stake center, with bundles of wood stacked around it.*

AT RISE: COURTIERS, CLARENCE, KING ARTHUR, *and* MERLIN *stand right and left, as* HANK *is dragged in right by* 1ST *and* 2ND GUARDS. CLARENCE *goes over to* HANK, *speaks to him quietly.*

CLARENCE *(To* HANK): My friend, it was through my efforts that the change was made for the day of your execution.

HANK: *Your* efforts? (GUARDS *tie* HANK *to stake and pile wood around him.*)

CLARENCE: Yes, and hard work it was, too. When I named your calamity, the King and all his court were stricken with terror. Then I had an idea. I told them that your power would not reach its peak until tomorrow, and that if they would save the sun, they must kill

you today while your magic is still working. In the frenzy of their fright, they swallowed my lie, and here you are!

HANK (*Miserably*): Clarence, how could you!

CLARENCE (*Excitedly*): You only need to make a *little* darkness, and the people will go mad with fear and set you free. They will take me for a featherheaded fool, and you will be made great! But I beg of you, spare our blessed sun, for me—your one true friend! (*Backs away into crowd*)

HANK (*Miserably*): My one, true, featherheaded friend! You have ruined me!

MERLIN (*Approaching* HANK, *waving his arms and sneering*): You call yourself a magician? Then stop the devouring flames if you can! I defy you! (*Beckons to* GUARD, *who comes forward with torch.* HANK *throws up his arms in an attitude of despair, and suddenly lights begin to dim. All gasp and look up.*)

COURTIERS (*Ad lib*): Look! The sun is disappearing! It's getting dark, and it's only noon! (*Etc.*)

HANK (*Looking up in surprise*): The eclipse! It's starting! I don't know where it came from, or how it happened, but I'd better make the most of it, or I'm done for! (*Strikes grand attitude, pointing upward*)

MERLIN (*Frantically*): Apply the torch!

KING ARTHUR: I forbid it! (MERLIN *snatches torch from* GUARD *and starts toward stake.*)

HANK: Stay where you are! If any man moves, even the King, I will blast him with thunder and lightning! (COURTIERS *step back.* MERLIN *hesitates, then hands torch to* GUARD, *and backs away.*)

KING ARTHUR (*To* HANK): Be merciful, fair sir. It was reported to us that your powers would not reach their full strength until tomorrow, but—

HANK: That report was a lie. My powers are at full strength *now!* (COURTIERS *crowd around* KING ARTHUR *frantically.*)

COURTIERS (*Ad lib*): Oh, save us! Give him whatever he wants! Do whatever he wants, only save the sun! (*Etc.*)

KING ARTHUR: Name your terms, reverend sir, but banish this calamity!

HANK (*Looking up*): Well ... I must have some time to consider.

KING ARTHUR: But it grows darker every moment!

COURTIERS (*Ad lib*): It's getting colder and colder! The night winds are blowing at noon! It's the end of the world! (*Etc.*)

HANK: Nevertheless, I must think! (*Looks up as lights continue to dim to almost complete darkness; to himself*) What *is* this? How am I to tell whether this is the sixth century or not with this eclipse coming a day early? (*Pulls sleeve of* 3RD GUARD) What day of the month is this?

3RD GUARD (*Stepping back, terrified*): The twenty-first, reverend sir.

HANK: The twenty-first! (*To himself*) That featherheaded Clarence told me today was the twentieth! (*With sigh of relief*) But his mistake about the date, and his good intentions in changing my day of execution, have saved me after all! I'm in King Arthur's court, all right, and there's only one course for me to take. (*Turns to* KING) Sir King, whether or not I blot out the sun forever, or restore it, is up to you. You shall remain King and receive all the glories and honors that belong to you. But you must appoint me your perpetual minister, and give me one percent of all increases in revenue I may create for the state.

KING ARTHUR: It shall be done! Away with his bonds! Do him homage, all of you, for he is now at my right hand and clothed with power and authority! Now, sweep away this darkness and bring the light again.

(GUARDS *untie* HANK.)

HANK *(To himself):* I wish I knew how long this eclipse is supposed to last! *(To KING)* Sir King, I may be clothed in power and authority in your eyes, but in my eyes, I am practically naked. I must have my clothes back.

KING ARTHUR: They are not good enough. Bring him costly garments! Clothe him like a prince! (KING *claps his hands several times, and* SERVANTS *rush in with rich robe, plumed hat, jeweled sword, etc., and start to put them on* HANK.)

HANK *(As he is being clothed):* Let it be known that I shall be called The Boss, and all who do as I say and don't get in my way will be spared any further calamities. *(Turning)* As for you, Merlin, beware! Your magic is weak, and I have knowledge of enchantments that can knock you out of commission forever!

MERLIN *(Menacingly):* You have not seen the last of me!

KING ARTHUR: Everything shall be as you say, Sir Boss, only bring back the sun!

CLARENCE *(On his knees):* For your one true friend's sake, bring back the sun!

HANK *(To himself):* I hope it's time. *(Solemnly lifts his arms and gazes upward)* Let the enchantment dissolve and pass harmlessly away! *(Darkness continues. The people stir uneasily. HANK waves his arms in grand flourish. Still it remains dark. HANK makes more flourishes, and slowly lights begin to come up, gradually becoming brighter and brighter. COURTIERS shout for joy.)*

CLARENCE: Oh, thank you, Sir Boss! You have worked a wondrous miracle, but I beg of you, never do it again!

HANK: Don't worry, Clarence, I won't perform this particular miracle again. Come, my boy, I'll find some suitable quarters in the castle and set up a factory. You can be my assistant, and I'll show you how to make all kinds of other miracles. *(Starts off left with his arm around CLARENCE's shoulders, then suddenly stops, scratching his head)* A Connecticut Yankee in King Arthur's Court! You know, a situation like this has all kinds of possibilities! And if I ever get back to Hartford, what a story I'll have to tell! *(Exits left with CLARENCE as COURTIERS bow to him, and curtain falls)*

Thinking About It

1. You are Boy. What questions will you ask Old Hank about this incident? And what will Old Hank tell you?

2. Plays need suspense if they're going to hold an audience without a rope. If you are directing this play, what three places in it will you try to provide suspense, and how?

3. You are being sent to King Arthur's England and, unfortunately, you aren't going there during an eclipse. But you may carry one item in your knapsack. What will it be? Tell the story of what happened to you.

NEIGHBORHOOD IMPROVEMENT

Eighteen-year-old Pedro Reyes gets things done. And he believes that other teens can too. This is his advice for other kids who want to do something for their community: "If they see something wrong, they can do something about it. Just get out there and do it."

Pedro, a high school senior from Los Angeles, is a member of Belmont High School's Youth Community Service Club. But you get the feeling from talking to Pedro that he'd be out working to improve his community whether he was a club member or not. And he believes one person can influence another. "Say I want to clean up trash from a neighborhood. I can talk to one person, and if he decides to do it, he tells someone. It's like a little chain. That person tells someone, and that person tells someone. . . ."

BY KATHY HENDERSON

A lot of Pedro's activities do begin in his club. The club meets every Friday during lunch. Anyone can suggest a project for the club to work on. The club has cleaned up neighborhoods, taught blind children, painted out graffiti, planted trees, and more.

Pedro has become their tree expert. He completed a special class to become a Citizen Forester, even though he was the only high school student in a class full of adults. To combat the greenhouse effect, he organized his club to plant trees at the high school and at a day care center. Pedro studied which kind of trees would be best for each site. The trees had to be able to withstand drought and have deep roots that wouldn't break through the con- crete. For the day care center, Pedro chose trees that would provide good shade for the children on hot days.

Pedro calls his club a melting pot. Club members include Latinos like Pedro as well as students with Chinese, Japanese, Cambodian, and Philippine heritage. They all work together when a project comes up.

"People really support us. We get a lot of paint and stuff donated. When we're out in a neighborhood working, people will come out and give us water and sodas. They'll start working, too. Gang members may come by and talk negative, but we ignore them."

There was a time when Pedro wasn't interested in community service or in school. "I almost got kicked out of school in junior high. I was hanging out with bad kids. But little by little I started to turn around. I decided that the purpose of my life was more than that. When I started high school I got a fresh start."

Pedro was shy when he first started his community service work. It was hard for him to approach people for help or to speak in front of a group. Because Pedro was determined to make a difference, he learned how to get things done. He figured out how to get permission from the Los Angeles School District to plant trees. He found out that there was paint available at city hall for community projects. Recently, Pedro received a national award for his volunteer work. With new confidence, he spoke to the thousands of people who were in the audience at the awards ceremony. He even appeared on the *Today* show.

Now Pedro is looking forward to college, a term in the Peace Corps, and a career in counseling. "There is no community service club at the college that I'm going to. I think I'm going to have to start one," says Pedro.

THINKING ABOUT IT

1. Is Pedro Reyes unusual or are many young people involved in community improvement? What evidence can you cite—from your own experience and from what you've heard or read?

2. What has Pedro learned from his work in the community? How has he changed?

3. What in your community would you like to see improved? What could you do to get these improvements? How would you encourage people to help you?

Your World
by Georgia Douglas Johnson

Your world is as big as you make it.
I know, for I used to abide
In the narrowest nest in a corner,
My wings pressing close to my side.

But I sighted the distant horizon
Where the skyline encircled the sea
And I throbbed with a burning desire
To travel this immensity.

I battered the cordons around me
And cradled my wings on the breeze
Then soared to the uttermost reaches
With rapture, with power, with ease!

Women
by Alice Walker

They were women then
My mama's generation
Husky of voice—Stout of
Step
With fists as well as
Hands
How they battered down
Doors
And ironed
Starched white
Shirts
How they led
Armies
Headragged Generals
Across mined
Fields
Booby-trapped
Ditches
To discover books
Desks
A place for us
How they knew what we
Must know
Without knowing a page
Of it
Themselves.

JANE ADDAMS
1860–1935

Halsted Street, Chicago. 1889. A blistering hot summer day.

Garbage is everywhere. The broken pavement is covered with spoiled fruits and vegetables, papers, bottles—rubbish of every kind. In places the garbage is several inches deep. The alleys running off Halsted Street, near Polk Street, smell like open sewers. The few real sewers are not attached to the broken-down wooden houses and dark, dirty tenement buildings that line the street. There are no toilets in the houses. Courtyards are thick with cockroaches—and crawling babies. Rats dart to and fro. In some of the basements, sheep are slaughtered. The smell hangs in the air. Oily rags collected from the city dump line the walls of rooms, covering cracks. There are no fire escapes. In dirty cellars under the sidewalk, bakers make bread. Tubs of milk stand uncovered to buzzing swarms of flies.

It was to this neighborhood that two well-dressed, attractive young ladies first came during

BY WILLIAM JAY JACOBS

the summer of 1889. Both of these young ladies were in their late twenties. They hoped—of all things—to rent a house on Halsted Street. Most well-dressed people wouldn't even go near such a street. Who were these women?

One was Jane Addams. The other was her good friend, Ellen Starr. As they made their way along the crowded sidewalks of Halsted Street, people scarcely noticed them. The two listened silently to the shouts and busy chatter of voices in many languages—Polish, Greek, German, Russian, Yiddish, Italian. At the time, three of every four Chicagoans were immigrants. Settlers from more than twenty nations lived in the Halsted Street neighborhood. There, on Halsted Street, the two ladies found a large old house that was just right for their purposes.

They were going to start a settlement house. It would be a place where poor people could learn to help themselves. If the idea worked in Chicago, it could work in other cities. And then America would be a better place.

Jane Addams and Ellen Starr called the house they had chosen Hull House. Along with the many women who later worked there, it would become famous throughout the world.

What was it that brought Jane Addams to Hull House? Why did she decide to spend her life helping others?

As a child Jane Addams often was ill. She was born with a crooked back and walked with her head to one side. It was painful for her to ride horseback, and she could not run and play with other children. Instead she read much and thought much. Early pictures show her as a serious child with sad, dreamy eyes.

Photo courtesy of the Chicago Historical Society ▶

Still, she had a comfortable childhood. Her wealthy father owned a flour mill and a sawmill in a small Illinois town. A well-known man in the state, Addams served in the state legislature and at one time even was considered for the governorship.

Jane adored her father. She believed everything he said. She even tried to copy his ways of speech. Since he awoke before dawn to read for several hours, so did she. Thinking herself ugly, she did not want to be seen in public with her father. Jane did not like to feel that "strange people should know my handsome father owned such a homely little girl."

As early as the age of six, Jane Addams thought about her responsibilities in life. Again and again she dreamed at night that she was the only person left on earth. Nothing could be done to start the business of the world again until someone made a wagon wheel. She knew it was a job that only she could do, but she did not know how.

Also at the age of six, she saw poor people for the first time. She learned that being poor had something to do with housing. It was then she promised herself that when she grew up she would go to the city. She would have a big house like her own. But it would not be alongside other big, beautiful houses. She would put it right in the middle of all the "horrid little houses."

Very few six-year-olds think the thoughts Jane Addams did. She was a very "different" kind of child.

At Rockford College in Illinois, Jane graduated with the highest grades in her class. But she did more than just study. She took part in almost every school activity. Although she was shy, she taught herself to be a good public speaker. Once she participated in a speaking contest with students from other colleges. Among the other contestants was a young man about whom the United States would hear much. His name was William Jennings Bryan. Neither Miss Addams nor Bryan won the speaking contest.

At Rockford Jane had a romance with a young man named Rollin Salisbury. He asked her to marry him. She refused. Later he became a famous professor at the University of Chicago. For many years he worked only six miles from Hull House in Chicago. Legend says that he never once stepped inside the door.

After graduating from college Jane Addams enrolled in medical school. She hoped to become a doctor and work among the poor, but after one year she had to drop out because of poor health. Her doctor suggested that travel and relaxation might help.

Miss Addams traveled through Europe. But she did not relax. She visited the slums of London. There she saw starving women and children clawing at each other to get at rotting food already marked "not fit to eat." It was a horrible sight. She never forgot it.

While in London she visited a settlement house called Toynbee Hall. Workers could go there at night for classes. Children could play games. Students from Oxford University were in charge of Toynbee Hall. Even though the Oxford men were from wealthy families, they wanted to do something for less fortunate people.

That seemed important to Jane Addams. As the daughter of a wealthy man she had been allowed to get an education. But as a woman she was not really expected to do anything with it.

Was her life worth much, she asked, if she could not do anything with her knowledge? Suddenly, while watching a bullfight in Madrid, Spain, she decided to stop just thinking about helping the poor and actually do something. She would fight!

At that moment in Madrid, she saw in her mind exactly what she would do with her life. She would give other wealthy young women a chance to use their educations, just as the Oxford men had used theirs at Toynbee Hall in London.

Miss Addams returned to America. Just before her twenty-first birthday, her father had died. He had left her an inheritance. She saved all of that money and still had enough extra of her own to begin looking in Chicago for the house she needed to begin her work.

The house she found was Hull House. It had belonged to a wealthy real-estate man named Charles J. Hull, who once had been a penniless orphan boy. He had never forgotten the days of his childhood and had always tried to help the poor. When Jane Addams and Ellen Starr discovered Hull House, the ground floor was being used as a saloon, the second floor as a furniture factory.

At his death Charles Hull had willed the house to his niece. She first rented one floor of it to Jane Addams, then later leased the entire house to her, free of charge.

In September, 1889, Jane Addams and Ellen Starr joyfully moved into Hull House, bringing with them their own furniture and works of art.

At first the people of Halsted Street were suspicious of the two well-dressed women. Why would wealthy young ladies want to live in such a slum? Gradually Miss Addams and Miss Starr proved that they wanted only to be good neighbors and friends.

They began by setting up a reading room and a kindergarten. Many years later one of the first "guests" remembered "the soft words of the women of Hull House, the only soft and kind words we immigrant boys heard in those days."

Before long, Jane Addams busied herself with many things—washing newborn babies, taking care of children, nursing the sick, arranging for funerals, helping single working girls find clean, safe places to live.

Ellen Starr loved art. Because of her work, a wealthy Chicago merchant presented a gift of five thousand dollars to Hull House for the building of an art gallery. That was important to Jane Addams, too. She and Miss Starr both believed that human beings could not live in the ugliness of factories and slums. Surrounded by all that ugliness they would become less human, more like animals, unless somehow they could keep their love of beauty. Art was not just a frill. It was at the heart of what they were trying to do.

Shortly after the art gallery was built, the ladies opened a public kitchen. There the people of the neighborhood could buy good, nourishing food at low prices. They learned how to cook better and how to spend their food money wisely. But the immigrants were far more interested in books and paintings than in the kitchen. They flocked to the art gallery. They came in great numbers to the reading room.

One immigrant boy who later became a writer remembered that Hull House "was the first house I had ever been in where books and magazines just lay around as if there were plenty of them in the world."

It was hard for people living on Halsted Street to remember the beauty of nature. All around them they saw concrete and ugliness. So Jane Addams arranged for the children to go to camps along Lake Michigan. She also planned trips to the country for the adults. Some of the adults did not know there were lovely places in America. They thought the whole nation was like the streets of Chicago.

As the newspapers began to write about Hull House, many wealthy young women were drawn there. Like Jane Addams and Ellen Starr, they wanted to do their share in making a better world. And they had the education and free time to do something about it.

With more helpers the activities of Hull House grew. There was a playground for children—the first one in Chicago—so that youngsters would not have to play in the streets. There were clubs and classes for young people who had to work and could not go to high school. There was a music school. There was a nursery where working mothers could leave their children during the day. People were asked to pay a small amount of money for these services so they would not feel they were taking charity. The idea of Hull House was not to give charity but to help people to help themselves.

Older immigrants had a particularly hard time in America. What could they do in a country where so much of the work was done by machines? At Hull House Jane Addams gave them rooms where they could work on the crafts of their native lands—spinning, weaving, carving, metalworking, rug making. Then they could sell their products.

Before Miss Addams ever launched her work at Hull House, she underwent surgery to straighten her back. At that time the doctor told her she would never be able to have children of her own. Perhaps because of that, she always had a special place in her heart for the children of Halsted Street. Often she told of an incident when several little girls surprised her by refusing to take candy she wanted to give them. She learned that they had been working for weeks in a candy factory, six days a week from 7 A.M. to 9 P.M., and could not stand the sight of candy. Miss Addams fought hard to win passage of a law putting an end to child labor. Finally, in 1903, she won. The law that halted child labor in Illinois was almost entirely the work of Jane Addams.

She also attacked the problem of children in the prisons. Children accused of even minor crimes customarily were thrown into jail with tough, hardened criminals. Instead of learning to be better citizens, the children often emerged from prison ready for a life of crime. Jane Addams helped establish special juvenile courts, just for youthful offenders. Often she convinced judges not to send children to jail but to put them in her care.

Hull House became a place where anyone in trouble could come. And they came by the thousands—murderers and thieves, or simply young girls who could not afford to buy "proper" wedding dresses. Jane Addams and the women who worked with her never turned anyone away.

The story of Hull House became known throughout the United States, as did the reputation of Jane Addams. Miss Addams often was asked to help with other causes in the field of human rights. She helped, for example, to win passage of an amendment to the Constitution giving women the right to vote. Leaders such as Susan B. Anthony and Carrie Chapman Catt led the way, but Jane Addams also played an important part in winning adoption of the amendment.

Always she was interested in the problem of war. She hated war and thought that women could do much to put an end to it. In this she was disappointed. But she never stopped trying. Even after the United States entered World War I, she refused to admit that the purpose of the war was just. To her, peace was more important than winning any war—no matter how right the reasons for fighting might appear.

At the age of sixty-five, she still worked fourteen, sixteen, even eighteen hours a day. She traveled and gave speeches throughout the world. Every day she worked until she became too dizzy to work anymore.

In her old age she received many honors. Fourteen universities gave her honorary degrees. She received cash awards of as much as twenty-six thousand dollars in a single year, but she kept none of the money for herself. Finally, in 1931, a telegram arrived, telling her of the greatest honor of all—the Nobel Peace Prize. She gave the entire sixteen-thousand-dollar prize to the International League for Peace and Freedom, a group that was trying to put an end to all wars.

The years that followed were quiet ones for Jane Addams. One by one, the women of Hull House died. Then, finally, on May 21, 1935, Jane Addams herself, by then aged and ill, died peacefully in her sleep.

For hours thousands filed past her coffin to say good-bye to the small woman with the crooked back. One little child was heard to say, "Are we all Aunt Jane's children?" And in a way, they were.

In her lifetime Jane Addams had made few personal enemies. She tried to understand even those who opposed her. She shamed politicians into having the garbage cleaned from the streets of Chicago. Factory owners were certain they would go broke if they could not hire children to work for only a few pennies an hour. Jane Addams tried to understand even those men.

Some people consider the methods of someone like Jane Addams too slow in "ridding the world of evil." Change, they think, must be rapid, sweeping. But Jane Addams always knew that even "evil" people do not think they are evil. That is why she was willing to listen, to learn, and to understand the other person. Her way of working for a better world, although perhaps less dramatic or exciting, often achieves more lasting change in people's lives.

PULLING IT ALL TOGETHER

1. What would you have done if you'd worked at Hull House? What might you have learned?

2. Which of the selections in this book are you most likely to remember for a long while? Suppose that some day you say "Reading that selection affected my life." Which one would you be talking about? Why?

3. This book is called *Without a Map*. Why? Which characters in it began and ended "without a map"? Which began without a map but somehow charted or mapped their way?

BOOKS TO ENJOY

Sister
by Eloise Greenfield
Harper, 1974
Leafing through her diary, Doretha remembers the past four years when her father was still with the family, when she got along with her sister, when her mother smiled with her high dimples. What has gone wrong? Are Doretha and her sister headed for trouble?

Here at the Scenic-Vu Motel
by Thelma Hatch Wyss
Harper, 1988

Because the board of education of Pine Valley High School won't pay for a bus to make the three-hour, daily round trip to Bear Flats, Jake and six other students from Bear Flats are living at the Scenic-Vu Motel this school year. They decide on two rules: 1. Study hard. 2. Have fun. Can they do both?

Men in Armor:
The Story of Knights and Knighthood
by Richard Suskind
Peter Bendrick, 1990
Imagine yourself seven years old and being sent to a neighboring baron's castle to begin your training for knighthood! Many years later, after rigorous training, you are dubbed "Sir ———." Service and loyalty are now your only duties.

Bearstone

by Will Hobbs
Atheneum, 1989

In a last, desperate effort to find a place for Cloyd, his school sends him to work for an old rancher. The two get along, fight, make up, and finally plan a trip to the mountains to reopen the rancher's old gold mine. That trip only brings about more disasters for Cloyd! Will he ever overcome his loneliness and find a place to belong?

We Dare Not Go A-Hunting

by Charlotte MacLeod
Atheneum, 1980

Who kidnapped Annette Sotherby for the second time, along with Sammy Truell? Straight-headed islander Molly Bassett is unexpectedly and reluctantly on the case of these mysterious disappearances on Netaquid Island.

Park's Quest

by Katherine Paterson
Dutton, 1988

Park's search for his identity includes finding out about his father, who died in Vietnam. But no one will talk to him—not even his mother. One photograph and his father's favorite books are all he has to go on. Will going to visit his father's family—whom he has never seen—bring the truth?

LITERARY TERMS

Figurative Language Figurative language is language that goes beyond the ordinary meanings of words in order to emphasize ideas or emotions. When authors use **figures of speech,** they compare two different things in order to emphasize a similarity. The most common **figures of speech** are simile and metaphor. In "Not Your Average Freshman," the author says that the freshmen are herded onto the lawn "like a flock of sheep" (simile). Other **figurative language** includes the description of Mr. Darker as having "an icicle gaze" (metaphor), and Mrs. Cobb speaking in a voice "like fingernails scraping on a blackboard" (simile).

Point of View The **point of view** of a story is the author's choice of a narrator, or speaker, through whose eyes the story will be told. Often a story is told by a narrator who is not a character in the story and who uses pronouns such as "she," "he," "it," or "they" in the narration, as is the case in "Song of the Chirimia." This third person **point of view** lets the narrator report the speeches and actions of all the characters in the story. Sometimes the author chooses to have the story told by one of the characters in the story, who can reveal only personal thoughts and feelings and those things he or she sees or is told by other characters. This first person ("I") **point of view** is found in "Four O'Clock on Mondays and Thursdays."

Irony **Irony** is a contrast between what appears to be and what actually is or between what is expected or hoped for and what actually happens. Sometimes it has a surprise twist and sometimes it yields humor. Something that appears to have bad consequences actually may turn out for the good, or an apparently happy event may turn out to bring bad luck. In "Not Your Average Freshman," what appears to be disaster for Stanley keeps turning into spectacular success.

Legend A **legend** is an old story handed down by word of mouth that often tells about the great deeds of a hero. A **legend** may have some historical truth. *The Miraculous Eclipse,* involving King Arthur and Merlin, is a play based on the **legend** of King Arthur.

Myth A **myth** is an old story handed down from person to person and region to region, often by professional storytellers. Several versions of the same basic story often exist. Myths usually explain something about nature, suggesting that the interactions of gods, humans, and natural forces are responsible for natural phenomena. *The Arrow and the Lamp: The Story of Psyche* is a Greek myth that explains how a mortal became one of the gods. Butterflies are a reminder to mortals of Psyche and her undying love.

GLOSSARY

Vocabulary from your selections

ac cent (ak′sent), *n.* a characteristic manner of pronunciation heard in a particular section or locality of a country, or in the speech of a person speaking a language not his or her own: *a Southern accent, a foreign accent.*

al ter nate (ôl′tər nāt, al′tər nāt), *v.,* **-nat ed, -nat ing,** *—v.t.* **1** arrange, do, or perform (two things) each after the other continuously: *alternate work and pleasure.* **2** interchange regularly: *alternate two hours of work with one hour of rest.*

a mend ment (ə mend′mənt), *n.* change made or offered in a law, bill, or motion by addition, omission, or alteration of language. The Constitution of the United States has over twenty amendments.

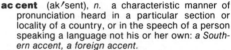

bide (bīd), *v.,* **bid ed** or **bode, bid ed, bid ing.** *—v.i.* remain or continue in some state or action; wait.

black smith (blak′smith′), *n.* person who works with iron by heating it in a forge and hammering it into shape on an anvil. Blacksmiths mend tools and also make and fit horseshoes.

cacao The **cacao** pod has **cacao** seeds inside.

ca ca o (kə kā′ō, kə kä′ō), *n., pl.* **-ca os.** **1** a small, tropical American evergreen tree grown for its large, nutritious seeds. **2** also **cacao beans,** the seeds of this tree, which are fermented, then washed to remove the sticky coating, and dried, used especially in making cocoa and chocolate.

ca lam i ty (kə lam′ə tē), *n., pl.* **-ties.** **1** a great misfortune, such as a flood, a fire, the loss of one's sight or hearing. **2** serious trouble; misery.

chis el (chiz′əl), *n.* a cutting tool with a sharp edge at the end of a strong blade, used to cut or shape wood, stone, or metal.

com bat (kəm bat′, kom′bat), *v.,* **-bat ed, -bat ing** or **-bat ted, -bat ting.**—*v.t.* **1** fight against; oppose in battle. **2** struggle against.

cub by hole (kub′ē hōl′), *n.* a small, enclosed space.

drought The long **drought** had ruined the farm.

de cent (dē′snt), *adj.* **1** proper and right; suitable: *The decent thing to do is to pay for the damage you have done.* **2** modest; free from vulgarity; not obscene. **3** having a good reputation; respectable: *decent people.* **4** good enough; fairly good: *I get decent marks at school.*

drought (drout), *n.* **1** a long period of dry weather; continued lack of rain. **2** lack of moisture; dryness.

dun geon (dun′jən), *n.* 1 a dark underground room or cell to keep prisoners in. 2 donjon.

eas y go ing (ē′zē gō′ing), *adj.* taking matters easily; not worrying.

e clipse (i klips′), *n.* 1 a complete or partial blocking of light passing from one heavenly body to another. A **solar eclipse** occurs when the moon passes between the sun and the earth. A **lunar eclipse** occurs when the moon enters the earth's shadow. 2 loss of importance or reputation.

en chant ment (en chant′mənt), *n.* 1 use of magic or sorcery. 2 a magic spell.

ep ox y (e pok′sē), *adj.* of or designating a large group of compounds containing oxygen as a bridge between two different atoms or radicals in a chain. Epoxy resins are used in the manufacture of plastics, adhesives, etc.

e qua tion (i kwā′zhən, i kwā′shən), *n.* statement of the equality of two quantities. EXAMPLES: $(4 \times 8) + 12 = 44$. $C = 2\pi r$.

ex e cu tion (ek′sə kyü′shən), *n.* 1 a carrying out (of a plan, purpose, command, etc.); doing. 2 a putting into effect; enforcing. 3 way of carrying out or doing; degree of skill in executing something. 4 manner of performing or playing a piece of music. 5 a putting to death according to a legal sentence or decree.

frosh (frosh), *n., pl.* **frosh.** INFORMAL. freshman at a college or school.

graf fi ti (grə fō′tē), *n. pl.* of **graf fi to** (grə fē′tō) 1 drawings or writings scratched or scribbled on a wall or other surface. 2 INFORMAL. a single such drawing or writing.

har mo ny (här′mə nē), *n., pl.* **-nies.** 1 agreement of feeling, ideas, or actions; getting on well together: *The two brothers lived and worked in perfect harmony.* 2 an orderly or pleasing arrangement of parts; going well together; congruity: *In a beautiful landscape there is harmony of the different colors.* 3 the sounding together of musical tones in a chord. 4 structure of a piece of music in relation to the chords of which it consists, as distinguished from melody and rhythm. 5 study of chords in music and relating them to successive chords. 6 sweet or musical sound; music.

haze (hāz), *v.t.,* **hazed, haz ing.** force (freshmen, fraternity initiates, etc.) to do humiliating or ridiculous tasks; bully. —**haz′er,** *n.*

her ald (her′əld), *n.* 1 (formerly) an official who carried messages, made announcements, arranged and supervised tournaments and other public ceremonies, and regulated the use of armorial bearings. 2 person who carries messages and makes announcements; messenger.

im i tate (im′ə tāt), *v.t.,* **-tat ed, -tat ing.** 1 try to be like or act like; follow the example of: *The little boy imitated his older brother.* 2 make or do something

a hat	oi oil
ā age	ou out
ä far	u cup
e let	u̇ put
ē equal	ü rule
ėr term	
i it	ch child
ī ice	ng long
o hot	sh she
ō open	th thin
ô order	ᴛʜ then
	zh measure

$$\text{ə} = \begin{cases} \text{a in about} \\ \text{e in taken} \\ \text{i in pencil} \\ \text{o in lemon} \\ \text{u in circus} \end{cases}$$

< = derived from

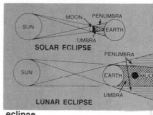

eclipse

impressionism

like; copy: *A parrot imitates the sounds it hears.*
3 act like: *She amused the class by imitating a baby, an old woman, and a bear.* **4** be like; look like; resemble: *wood painted to imitate stone.* [< Latin *imitatum* imitated, related to *imago* image]

im pa tient (im pā′shənt), *adj.* **1** not patient; not willing to put up with delay, opposition, pain, bother, etc: *She is impatient with her little sister.* **2** uneasy and eager; restless: *The horses are impatient to start the race.* **3** showing lack of patience; cross: *impatient answer.*

im pres sion ism (im presh′ə niz ′əm), *n.* style of painting developed by French painters of the late 1800's, characterized by the use of strong, bright colors applied in dabs to convey the impression of light striking and reflecting from a surface, rather than a photographic reproduction of the surface.

im pres sion ist (im presh′ə nist), *n.* artist, writer, or composer who practices impressionism.

in te grate (in′tə grāt), *v.,* -grat ed, -grat ing. —*v.t.* **1** make into a whole; complete. **2** put or bring together (parts) into a whole. **3** make (schools, parks, etc.) available to people of all races on an equal basis: *integrate a neighborhood.*

in te gra tion (in′tə grā′shən), *n.* **1** act or process of integrating. **2** inclusion of people of all races on an equal basis in schools, parks, neighborhoods, etc.

lib e ra tion (lib′ə rā′shən), *n.* **1** a setting free. **2** a being set free.

mel an chol y (mel′ən kol ′ē), *adj.* **1** depressed in spirits; sad; gloomy. **2** causing sadness; depressing: *a melancholy scene.* **3** lamentable; deplorable: *a melancholy fact.* **4** soberly thoughtful; pensive.

mi rac u lous (mə rak′yə ləs), *adj.* **1** constituting a miracle; contrary to or independent of the known laws of nature; supernatural. **2** marvelous; wonderful: *miraculous good fortune.* **3** producing miracles; having the power to work miracles.

mor tal (môr′tl), *adj.* **1** sure to die sometime; destined to undergo death. **2** of human beings; of mortals: *Mortal bodies feel pain.* —*n.* **1** a being that is sure to die sometime. All living creatures are mortals. **2** human being. [< Latin *mortalis* < *mortem* death]

neg a tive (neg′ə tiv), *adj., n.* —*adj.* **1** stating that something is not so; answering no to a question put or implied. **2** arguing against a question being formally debated: *the negative side.* **3** not positive: *negative suggestions.* —*n.* **1** word or statement that denies or negates.

nurs er y (nėr′sər ē), *n., pl.* -er ies. **1** room set apart for the use and care of babies. **2** a place where babies and small children are cared for during the day: *a day nursery.*

ogre The ogre was looking for his next meal.

o gre (ō′gər), *n.* **1** (in folklore and fairy tales) giant or monster that supposedly eats people. **2** person like such a monster in appearance or character.

o ra cle (ôr′ə kəl, or′ə kəl), *n.* **1** (in ancient Greece and Rome) an answer believed to be given by a god through a priest or priestess to some question. It often had a hidden meaning that was ambiguous or hard to understand. **2** place where the god was believed to give such answers. A famous oracle was at Delphi. **3** the priest, priestess, or other means by which the god's answer was believed to be given.

o ver due (ō′vər dü′, ō′vər dyü′), *adj.* more than due; due some time ago but not yet arrived, paid, etc.: *The train is overdue. This bill is overdue.*

pact (pakt), *n.* agreement between persons or parties; compact; treaty.

reign (rān), *n.* **1** period of power of a ruler: *Queen Victoria's reign lasted sixty-four years.* **2** act of ruling; royal power; rule: *The reign of a wise ruler benefits a country.* **3** existence everywhere; prevalence.

re un ion (rē yü′nyən), *n.* **1** a coming together again. **2** a being reunited. **3** a social gathering of persons who have been separated or who have interests in common: *a college reunion.*

rev e nue (rev′ə nü, rev′ə nyü), *n.* **1** money coming in; income: *The government gets revenue from taxes.* **2** a particular item of income. **3** a source of income.

sa loon (sə lün′), *n.* **1** place where alcoholic drinks are sold and drunk; tavern. **2** a large room for general or public use: *The ship's passengers ate in the dining saloon.*

satch el (sach′əl), *n.* a small bag for carrying clothes, books, etc.; handbag.

scribe (skrīb), *n.* person who copies manuscripts. Before printing was invented, there were many scribes.

set tle ment house, (set′l mənt hous), *n.* place in a poor, neglected neighborhood where work for its improvement is carried on.

skew er (skyü′ər), *n.* **1** a long pin of wood or metal stuck through meat to hold it together while it is cooking. **2** something shaped or used like a long pin. —*v.t.* **1** fasten with a skewer or skewers. **2** pierce with or as if with a skewer.

suit or (sü′tər), *n.* **1** man who is courting a woman. **2** person bringing suit in a court of law. **3** anyone who sues or petitions.

vile (vīl), *adj.,* **vil er, vil est.** **1** very bad: *vile weather.* **2** foul; disgusting; obnoxious: *a vile smell.* **3** evil; low; immoral: *vile habits.* **4** poor; mean; lowly: *the vile tasks of the kitchen.* **5** of little worth or account; trifling. —**vile′ly,** *adv.* —**vile′ness,** *n.*

vol un teer (vol′ən tir′), *n.* **1** person who enters military or other service of one's own free will; one who is not drafted. **2** person who serves without pay. In some towns, the fire department is made up of volunteers. —*adj.* **1** of or made up of volunteers: *volunteer fire company.* **2** serving as a volunteer; *a volunteer firefighter.*

a hat	oi oil
ā age	ou out
ä far	u cup
e let	u̇ put
ē equal	ü rule
ėr term	
i it	ch child
ī ice	ng long
o hot	sh she
ō open	th thin
ô order	ᴛʜ then
	zh measure

ə = { a in about / e in taken / i in pencil / o in lemon / u in circus }

< = derived from

scribe The **scribe** was at work on a manuscript.

ACKNOWLEDGMENTS

Text

Page 7: "Not Your Average Freshman" from *The Fantastic Freshman* by Bill Brittain. Copyright © 1988 by Bill Brittain. Reprinted by permission of HarperCollins Publishers.

Page 23: "The War of the Wall" by Toni Cade Bambara. Reprinted by permission of the author.

Page 37: "Outdoor Art in America" by Toni Cade Bambara. Copyright © by Toni Cade Bambara, 1991.

Page 41: From *Going Home* by Nicholasa Mohr. Copyright © 1986 by Nicholasa Mohr. Used by permission of Dial Books for Young Readers.

Page 64: "Celebrate Our Differences" by Nicholasa Mohr. Copyright © by Nicholasa Mohr, 1991.

Page 69: *Song of the Chirimia* retold by Jane Anne Volkmer. Copyright © 1990 by Carolrhoda Books, Inc., 241 First Avenue North, Minneapolis, MN 55401. Used by permission of the publisher.

Page 77: *The Arrow and the Lamp: The Story of Psyche* retold by Margaret Hodges. Illustrated by Donna Diamond. Text copyright © 1989 by Margaret Hodges. Illustrations copyright © 1989 by Donna Diamond. By permission of Little, Brown and Company.

Page 89: "The Land of Mount Olympus" by Margaret Hodges. Copyright © by Margaret Hodges, 1991.

Page 93: "The Miraculous Eclipse" from *A Connecticut Yankee in King Arthur's Court* by Mark Twain from *Stage Plays from the Classics* by Joellen Bland. Copyright © 1987 by Joellen Bland. Reprinted by permission of Plays, Inc.

Page 115: "Neighborhood Improvement" from *What Would We Do Without You?* by Kathy Henderson. Copyright © 1990 by Kathy Henderson. Reprinted by permission of Betterway Publications, Inc.

Page 121: "Women" from *Revolutionary Petunias and Other Poems* by Alice Walker. Copyright © 1970 by Alice Walker. Reprinted by permission of Harcourt Brace Jovanovich, Inc.

Page 123: "Jane Addams" from *Great Lives: Human Rights* by William Jay Jacobs. Copyright © 1990 by William Jay Jacobs. Reprinted with permission of Charles Scribner's Sons, an imprint of Macmillan Publishing Company.

Artists

Illustrations owned and copyrighted by the illustrator.
Scott Morgan: Cover, 1, 3–5, 138, 139
Mary Grant Pré: 6, 12, 17, 21
Tom Tomita: 22, 26, 31, 32, 33, 34–35, 39
Ruben Ramos: 40, 45, 48, 53, 55, 60, 67
John Martinez: 68–69, 71, 73, 75
Donna Diamond: 76–77, 83, 87, 88, 91
Rob Day: 92–93, 96, 101, 103, 107, 108, 113
Thom Sevalrud: 120–121

Photographs

Page 36: Courtesy of Toni Cade Bambara
Page 65: Courtesy of Nicholasa Mohr
Page 88: Courtesy of Margaret Hodges
Pages 114, 116, 118: Courtesy Constitutional Rights Foundation
Page 122: University of Illinois at Chicago/Jane Addams Memorial Collection at Hull House
Pages 125, 130: Chicago Historical Society

Glossary

The contents of the Glossary entries in this book have been adapted from Scott Foresman *Advanced Dictionary*, copyright © 1988 by Scott, Foresman and Company.

Page 140 (top): U.S. Department of Agriculture; Page 140 (bottom): Library of Congress; Page 142 (top): "Two Dancers," Edgar Degas, Amy McCormick Memorial, Courtesy of The Art Institute of Chicago; Page 142 (bottom): From the collection of Gay Russell-Dempsey; Page 143: Staatsbibliothek, Bremen
Unless otherwise acknowledged, all photographs are the property of Scott-Foresman.